"MASTER YODA...

...DO YOU REALLY THINK...

"...IT WILL COME TO WAR?"

STAR WARS®
BATTLES
FOR THE GALAXY

WRITTEN BY
DANIEL WALLACE

CONTENTS

When Emperor Palpatine builds the most powerful battle station the galaxy has ever seen, it seems as though the Sith have triumphed. But in every battle there are heroes: Heroes who will fight even if they are outnumbered. Heroes who will attack a weapon as dangerous as the Death Star to restore freedom to the galaxy.

22 BBY: Battle of Geonosis

19 BBY: Birth of Luke and Leia

19 BBY: Jedi Purge

41 BBY: Birth of Anakin

32 BBY: Battle of Naboo

50 BBY **40 BBY** **30 BBY** **20 BBY**

REPUBLIC ERA

THE CLONE WARS

TIMES OF WAR

Throughout the galaxy, great conflicts have been decided on the battlefield. No one wants war, but sometimes fighting is necessary to free people who are suffering, or to defeat an evil tyrant. The Jedi Knights, the Republic's clone army, and the Rebel Alliance all fight hard to defeat powerful enemies through warfare.

So who are these skilled soldiers? What secrets do they know about combat on unfamiliar planets and in the emptiness of outer space? And how can they make you ready to face your own foes? Take a seat, Recruit, and prepare for your mission briefing!

NOTE ON DATES: Dates are fixed around the Battle of Yavin in year 0. All events prior to this are measured in terms of years Before the Battle of Yavin (BBY). Events after it are measured in terms of years After the Battle of Yavin (ABY).

0 Battle of Yavin   3 ABY Battle of Hoth

2 BBY Rebel   4 ABY Battle of Endor
Alliance is
founded

10 BBY   **0**   **10 ABY**   **20 ABY**

EMPIRE ERA   NEW REPUBLIC ERA

REPUBLIC

The Republic is a democracy. It aims to govern life in the galaxy freely and fairly. Every planet has a vote and the chance to voice its opinion. But some members of the Republic have other ideas...

JEDI ORDER

The Jedi are the peacekeepers of the galaxy. They work together with the rulers of the Republic to ensure that laws are being obeyed. After the Clone Wars, the surviving Jedi join the Rebel Alliance.

SENATE

The Senate is the government of the Republic. Some Senators join the Separatists, and the Senate later becomes part of the Empire.

Senators who oppose the Empire join the Rebels.

CLONE ARMY

The Republic controls a huge army of clone troopers. When the Empire later takes control, the clone troopers become stormtroopers.

CHANCELLOR

Chancellor Palpatine is the leader of the Republic. He directs the Senate and tries to keep the galaxy peaceful. But he is hiding a dark secret...

REBELS

LUKE SKYWALKER

Luke is the last remaining Jedi. He joins the Rebels, and leads them in their fight against the Empire.

LEIA ORGANA

Princess Leia is a daring Senator. She does not agree with the ideals of the Empire so she joins the Rebel Alliance.

HAN SOLO

Han Solo is a smuggler. At first he helps the Rebels for money, but he later joins the Alliance and fights for its cause.

When the Republic becomes the Empire, those who decide to resist the evil Emperor join the Rebel Alliance.

Battles rage across the galaxy. Governments rise and fall. The Clone Wars saw the Republic ravaged by the Separatists—and turned into the Empire. Use this page to learn about the people and organizations that have shaped the history of the galaxy, for good or for evil.

SEPARATISTS

There are some people who believe the Republic is corrupt. They want to take control of the galaxy. They call themselves the Confederacy of Independent Systems, or Separatists.

DARTH SIDIOUS
Chancellor Palpatine is really the Sith Lord Darth Sidious in disguise. Sidious manipulates both sides of the Clone Wars as part of his quest to turn the galaxy into an Empire.

TRADE FEDERATION
The Trade Federation is an organization that controls most of the trade in the galaxy. It is run by greedy Neimoidians who care only about making a profit.

APPRENTICE
Count Dooku is Darth Sidious's Sith apprentice. He leads the Separatists under Sidious's command. Dooku is killed when Sidious seeks a new, more powerful apprentice.

DROID ARMY
Built by the Trade Federation, the droid army fights for the Separatists. When the clone army joins the Empire, the droids are decommissioned.

EMPIRE

At the end of the Clone Wars, what's left of the Republic becomes the Empire—a tyrannical dictatorship ruled by a Sith: Emperor Palpatine.

EMPEROR
Darth Sidious installs himself as the Emperor—the chief ruler of the galaxy. He is a ruthless, deadly tyrant and is feared by all.

DARTH VADER
Jedi Anakin Skywalker turns to the dark side and becomes Darth Sidious's new apprentice, Darth Vader. Vader directs the Imperial Army.

IMPERIAL ARMY
The Republic clone army becomes the Imperial Army. Clone troopers are now stormtroopers and enforce Imperial rule across the galaxy.

DROID ARMY STATS

LEADER: COUNT DOOKU

ALLEGIANCE: SEPARATISTS

HEADQUARTERS: GEONOSIS

WEAPONS: BLASTER RIFLE, BLASTER PISTOL, THERMAL DETONATOR

VEHICLES: STAP, MTT, AAT, DROID TRI-FIGHTER

VALUES: OBEDIENCE TO PROGRAMMING

CHAIN OF COMMAND

DARTH SIDIOUS (IN SECRET)

COUNT DOOKU

GENERAL GRIEVOUS

COMMANDER BATTLE DROIDS

BATTLE DROIDS

Super battle droids have thick armor and blasters built into their arms. They aren't as common as regular battle droids but they are much harder to destroy.

RADIATION SENSORS TO SEE IN THE DARK

SUPER BATTLE DROID

DEADLY ROLLERS

Droidekas, or destroyer droids, have their own shield generators. They can also transform into a wheel and roll toward a target. They are so fast and powerful, they sometimes make Jedi Knights retreat!

TWIN RAPID-FIRE BLASTER CANNONS

DROIDEKAS

DROIDEKAS LOOK LIKE THEIR INSECTOID ALIEN BUILDERS

12

DROID IS DIRECTED FROM CENTRAL COMMAND SIGNAL

E-5 BLASTER

BATTLE DROID

Droid ARMY

FRAGILE CONSTRUCTION

The Separatists use droid soldiers to fight their battles. Droids never get tired, always obey orders, and can be easily replaced when damaged. Battle droids, super battle droids, and droidekas may not be very smart, but they can be deadly!

EXPENDABLE
B1 battle droids are the Separatists' foot soldiers. They are easy to defeat but can be dangerous if many attack at once. Droid commanders have yellow markings and are slightly more independently minded.

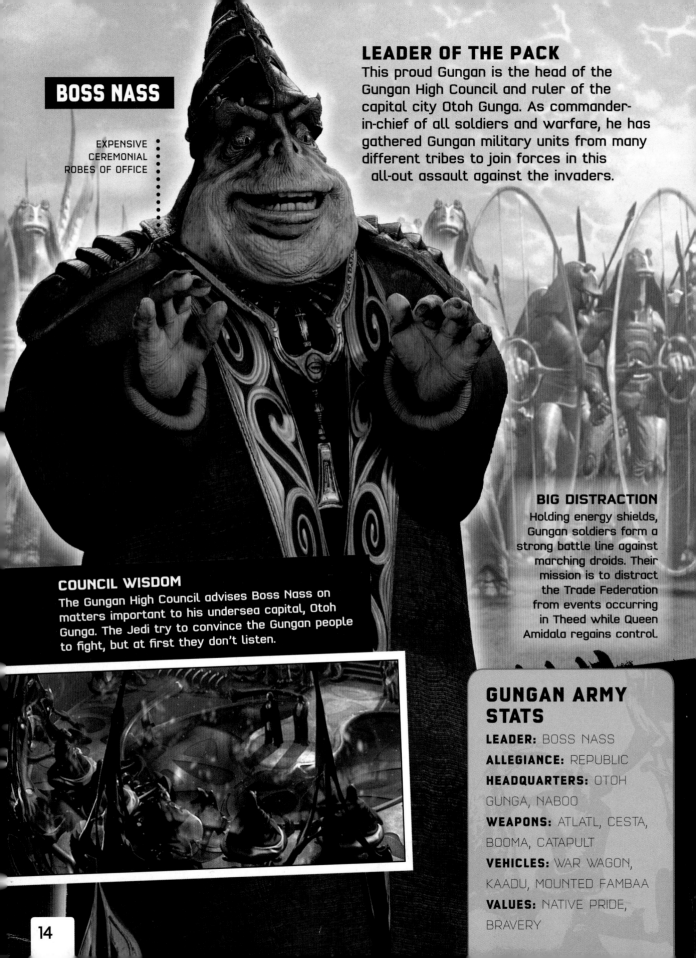

BOSS NASS

EXPENSIVE CEREMONIAL ROBES OF OFFICE

LEADER OF THE PACK

This proud Gungan is the head of the Gungan High Council and ruler of the capital city Otoh Gunga. As commander-in-chief of all soldiers and warfare, he has gathered Gungan military units from many different tribes to join forces in this all-out assault against the invaders.

BIG DISTRACTION

Holding energy shields, Gungan soldiers form a strong battle line against marching droids. Their mission is to distract the Trade Federation from events occurring in Theed while Queen Amidala regains control.

COUNCIL WISDOM

The Gungan High Council advises Boss Nass on matters important to his undersea capital, Otoh Gunga. The Jedi try to convince the Gungan people to fight, but at first they don't listen.

GUNGAN ARMY STATS

LEADER: BOSS NASS
ALLEGIANCE: REPUBLIC
HEADQUARTERS: OTOH GUNGA, NABOO
WEAPONS: ATLATL, CESTA, BOOMA, CATAPULT
VEHICLES: WAR WAGON, KAADU, MOUNTED FAMBAA
VALUES: NATIVE PRIDE, BRAVERY

MILITIAGUNGS USE
A STICK CALLED
AN ATLATL TO
THROW BLUE
PLASMA BALLS

PLASMA BALLS
(BOOMAS) ARE
MINED FROM
NABOO'S CORE

MILITIAGUNG

CHAIN OF COMMAND

BOSS NASS

BOMBAD GENERAL

GUNGAN OFFICERS

CAVALRY/MILITIAGUNGS

AMPHIBIOUS
GUNGANS DON'T
LIKE FIGHTING
ON LAND

Gungan
ARMY

The Naboo-dwelling Gungans have an
impressive army, but they don't plan on
fighting. However, when Queen Amidala informs
them that the Trade Federation's battle droids
are a threat to their entire planet, the Gungans
grab their weapons and prepare for action!

GUNGAN WEAPONS
Gungan warriors are also
known as militiagungs.
They use atlatls or long
sticks (called cestas) to
throw plasma balls
(boomas) into battle.
Some militiagungs ride
into battle on the
backs of animals
called kaadu.

15

BATTLE ANALYSIS: NABOO

PLANET: Naboo
LOCATION: Mid Rim
TERRAIN: Grassy plains, swamps, deep seas
INHABITANTS: Humans (the Naboo), Gungans
ALLEGIANCE: Republic

The Trade Federation, controlled by the Sith Lord Darth Sidious, has invaded the planet Naboo to provoke war. Although they are greatly outnumbered, Queen Amidala, her Royal Security Forces, two Jedi Knights, and the Gungan Jar Jar Binks unite to fight back. Working together, these allies hope to put an end to the invasion—a goal that requires six dangerous missions.

1. GRASSY PLAINS

OBJECTIVE:
Gungans to create a diversion for the droid army.

OUTCOME:
Battle begins, droids are successfully distracted.
MISSION COMPLETE.

2. THEED PALACE

OBJECTIVE:
Queen Amidala and her soldiers to sneak into the royal palace.

OUTCOME:
Team avoids battle droids and enters through window.
MISSION COMPLETE.

3. SPACE BATTLE

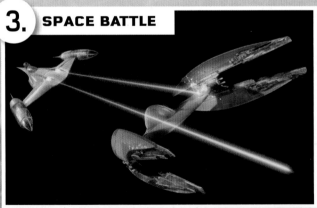

OBJECTIVE:
Naboo starfighter pilots to attack the Droid Control Ship.

OUTCOME:
Pilots engage hostile vulture droids, but suffer losses.
MISSION INCOMPLETE.

"This is a battle I do not think we can win."

**Captain Panaka,
Naboo Royal Security Forces**

BATTLE STATS

TRADE FEDERATION:
- SITH
- BATTLE DROIDS
- DROIDEKAS
- DROID CONTROL SHIP
- VULTURE DROIDS

PEOPLE OF NABOO:

- JEDI
- NABOO SOLDIERS
- GUNGAN ARMY
- NABOO N-1 STARFIGHTERS
- WEAPONS: LIGHTSABERS, BLASTERS, ENERGY BALLS

4. SITH DUEL

OBJECTIVE:
Jedi to eliminate the Sith Darth Maul.

OUTCOME:
Obi-Wan kills Maul, but Qui-Gon also dies. MISSION COMPLETE.

5. THEED THRONE ROOM

OBJECTIVE:
Queen Amidala to capture the Trade Federation viceroy, Nute Gunray.

OUTCOME:
Using a decoy, the Queen confuses the viceroy and makes him surrender. MISSION COMPLETE.

6. DROID CONTROL SHIP

OBJECTIVE:
Naboo pilots to destroy the Droid Control Ship.

OUTCOME:
Anakin blows up the ship from the inside, shutting down the droid army. MISSION COMPLETE.

CONSEQUENCES

The Battle of Naboo is a success for Naboo. Once again, the planet is under the rule of its Queen, and the Trade Federation has lost power. However, the battle sparks a crisis in the government of the Republic, and Palpatine becomes the new Chancellor. No one knows it yet, but this is his first step in leading the galaxy into an even bigger war.

Pieces of wrecked droids litter the battlefield. Jar Jar gets one stuck to his foot and just wants to shake it loose. As the enemy closes in from every side, Jar Jar's attempts to shake the robot off make it fire its weapon. First one battle droid goes down, then another, then another!

WHEN THE TRADE FEDERATION invades Naboo, the planet's inhabitants, the Gungans, are ready to fight. But Jar Jar Binks isn't so sure. This awkward Gungan misfit doesn't want to be a hero, let alone a General. When the battle begins, Jar Jar fumbles, bumbles, and panics—but somehow his antics destroy a large part of the enemy army!

WHAT GOOD IS CLUMSINESS ON THE BATTLEFIELD?

Hoping to escape from the blaster fire and explosions, Jar Jar tries to hitch a ride on a war wagon. His clumsiness causes the wagon to spill open, unleashing destructive plasma energy balls. These weapons conveniently collide with the attacking droids.

THE SEPARATISTS

The Separatist military has one major difference from other armies—it is made up almost entirely of droids. Many war machines that normally require pilots or drivers are replaced with big, specially designed robots. Droids attack in huge waves and can be replaced easily. The Separatists hope this is enough to bring them victory!

ARMORED ASSAULT TANK (AAT)
- **SIZE** 9.75 m (32 ft) LONG
- **SPEED** 55 km/hr (34 mph)
- **CAPACITY** 4 CREW, 6 BATTLE DROIDS ON EXTERIOR
- **WEAPONS** 1 HEAVY LASER CANNON, 2 SECONDARY LASER CANNONS, 6 PROJECTILE LAUNCHERS

CRAB DROID
- **SIZE** 1.49 m (4.9 ft) TALL
- **SPEED** 35 km/hr (22 mph)
- **CAPACITY** NONE
- **WEAPONS** TWIN BLASTER CANNONS, WATER JET SPRAYER

DROIDEKA (DESTROYER DROID)
- **SIZE** 1.83 m (6 ft) TALL
- **SPEED** 75 km/hr (47 mph)
- **CAPACITY** NONE
- **WEAPONS** 2 TWIN BLASTER CANNONS

MULTI-TROOP TRANSPORT (MTT)
- **SIZE** 31 m (101.7 ft) LONG
- **SPEED** 35 km/hr (22 mph)
- **CAPACITY** 4 CREW, 112 BATTLE DROIDS
- **WEAPONS** 4 TWIN BLASTER CANNONS

CORPORATE ALLIANCE TANK DROID
- **SIZE** 10 m (32.8 ft) LONG
- **SPEED** 50 km/hr (31 mph)
- **CAPACITY** NONE
- **WEAPONS** 2 LASER CANNONS, 2 ION CANNONS, MISSILE LAUNCHER

HAILFIRE DROID
- **SIZE** 6.8 m (22.3 ft) TALL
- **SPEED** 45 km/hr (28 mph)
- **CAPACITY** NONE
- **WEAPONS** 1 LASER CANNON, 2 MISSILE LAUNCHER ARRAYS

OCTUPTARRA DROID
- **SIZE** 14.6 m (48 ft) TALL
- **SPEED** 25 km/hr (16 mph)
- **CAPACITY** NONE
- **WEAPONS** 3 LASER CANNONS

SENSORS CAN SEE IN COMPLETE DARKNESS

DESTROYS ENEMY VEHICLES WITH ONE SHOT

LAND

DWARF SPIDER DROID
- **SIZE** 1.98 m (6.5 ft) TALL
- **SPEED** 30 km/hr (19 mph)
- **CAPACITY** NONE
- **WEAPONS** 1 HEAVY BLASTER CANNON

GOOD AT CROSSING ROUGH GROUND

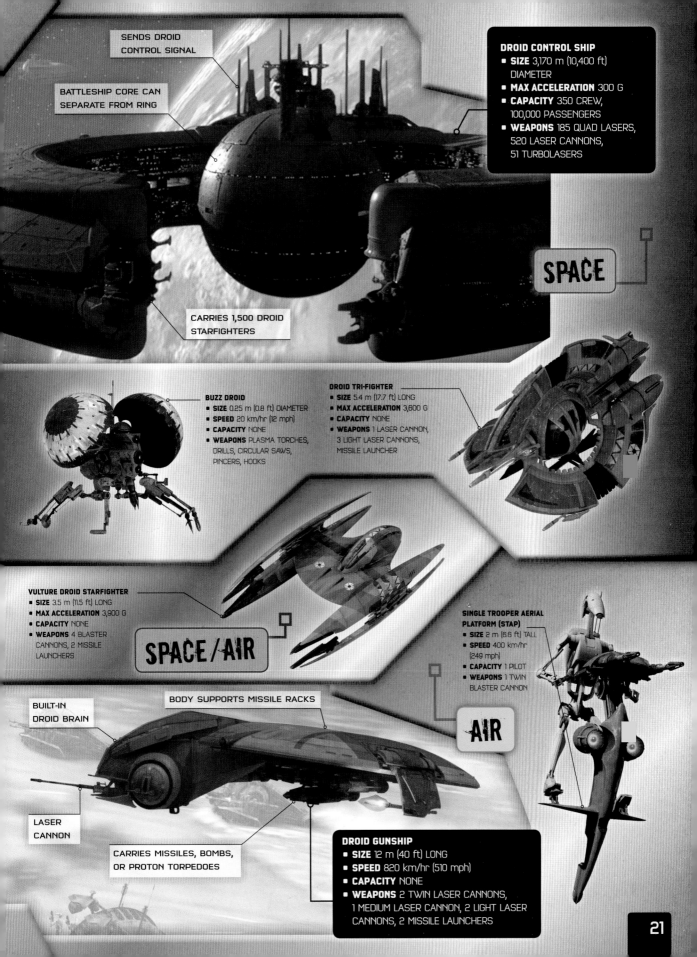

SENDS DROID CONTROL SIGNAL

BATTLESHIP CORE CAN SEPARATE FROM RING

CARRIES 1,500 DROID STARFIGHTERS

DROID CONTROL SHIP
- **SIZE** 3,170 m (10,400 ft) DIAMETER
- **MAX ACCELERATION** 300 G
- **CAPACITY** 350 CREW, 100,000 PASSENGERS
- **WEAPONS** 185 QUAD LASERS, 520 LASER CANNONS, 51 TURBOLASERS

SPACE

BUZZ DROID
- **SIZE** 0.25 m (0.8 ft) DIAMETER
- **SPEED** 20 km/hr (12 mph)
- **CAPACITY** NONE
- **WEAPONS** PLASMA TORCHES, DRILLS, CIRCULAR SAWS, PINCERS, HOOKS

DROID TRI-FIGHTER
- **SIZE** 5.4 m (17.7 ft) LONG
- **MAX ACCELERATION** 3,600 G
- **CAPACITY** NONE
- **WEAPONS** 1 LASER CANNON, 3 LIGHT LASER CANNONS, MISSILE LAUNCHER

VULTURE DROID STARFIGHTER
- **SIZE** 3.5 m (11.5 ft) LONG
- **MAX ACCELERATION** 3,900 G
- **CAPACITY** NONE
- **WEAPONS** 4 BLASTER CANNONS, 2 MISSILE LAUNCHERS

SPACE/AIR

SINGLE TROOPER AERIAL PLATFORM (STAP)
- **SIZE** 2 m (6.6 ft) TALL
- **SPEED** 400 km/hr (249 mph)
- **CAPACITY** 1 PILOT
- **WEAPONS** 1 TWIN BLASTER CANNON

BUILT-IN DROID BRAIN

BODY SUPPORTS MISSILE RACKS

AIR

LASER CANNON

CARRIES MISSILES, BOMBS, OR PROTON TORPEDOES

DROID GUNSHIP
- **SIZE** 12 m (40 ft) LONG
- **SPEED** 820 km/hr (510 mph)
- **CAPACITY** NONE
- **WEAPONS** 2 TWIN LASER CANNONS, 1 MEDIUM LASER CANNON, 2 LIGHT LASER CANNONS, 2 MISSILE LAUNCHERS

HOW CAN YOU STOP A DROID ARMY?

ON NABOO, Gungan warriors are bravely fighting the invading droid soldiers one at a time, but they are outnumbered. The droid army has one weakness: Every robot is controlled by a single huge ship floating above Naboo. A strike at the source of the droids' power could stop the army, but that's no easy task.

Anakin Skywalker is strong in the Force and a great Podracer pilot, but he has never flown a starfighter. However, Anakin isn't afraid. He has faced and overcome dangers on the Podracing track, and his confidence helps him join the other Naboo pilots in their daring fight.

The droid armies on the surface can't operate without a signal from their control ship. Thanks to Anakin's amazing shot, every droid soldier freezes in its tracks. The Gungan warriors are triumphant!

When Anakin fires two proton torpedoes at attacking droids, it accidentally starts a chain reaction that destroys the huge Droid Control Ship— he barely escapes the gigantic explosion!

JEDI GENERAL PLO KOON

THICK, PROTECTIVE SKIN

CHAIN OF COMMAND

JEDI GRAND MASTER

JEDI COUNCIL

JEDI GENERALS

JEDI COMMANDERS

CLONE TROOPERS

Jedi GENERALS

HIGH FLYER

During the Clone Wars, General Plo Koon develops a reputation as a fierce starship pilot. His loyalty to the clone troopers under his command is legendary.

Members of the Jedi Order study the secrets of the Force and use their wisdom to protect the galaxy. They would prefer to be peacekeepers rather than warriors, but when galactic peace is threatened, the Jedi are forced to take a more aggressive approach.

WAR FOR PEACE

In times of crisis, the Jedi Order must fight for justice and democracy. Jedi Knights and Masters become Generals, while Padawans become Commanders. During the Clone Wars, General Obi-Wan Kenobi oversees a legion of clone troopers. His second-in-command is Clone Commander Cody, with whom he develops a close bond.

A Jedi must be able to adapt to his military role at a moment's notice. For most members of the Jedi Council, the Battle of Geonosis is the very first time they assume the role of General.

MASTER OF LIGHTSABER COMBAT FORM III (SORESU)

JEDI GENERAL OBI-WAN KENOBI

STRATEGY MEETINGS
The Jedi Council directs the Republic's military effort. Using holoprojectors, any location can serve as a briefing room, including the Kashyyyk command center.

JEDI STATS

LEADER: YODA

ALLEGIANCE: REPUBLIC

HEADQUARTERS: JEDI TEMPLE, CORUSCANT

WEAPONS: LIGHTSABERS

VEHICLES: DELTA-7 STARFIGHTERS, ETA-2 INTERCEPTORS

VALUES: JUSTICE, HONOR, DEMOCRACY, INTEGRITY

BATTLE ANALYSIS:
GEONOSIS

PLANET: Geonosis
LOCATION: Remote sector of Outer Rim
TERRAIN: Dusty, rocky, with spire hives
INHABITANTS: Insectoid Geonosians
ALLEGIANCE: Separatists

New information from Obi-Wan Kenobi has revealed that the Separatists—led by Count Dooku—have built an enormous droid army. The Republic has access to a secret army of clones. When Obi-Wan is captured by Count Dooku, the Galactic Senate and the Jedi Council agree to take decisive action. The Republic sends envoys and troops to Geonosis, with orders to undertake six crucial missions.

1. DROID FACTORY

OBJECTIVE:
Anakin Skywalker and Padmé Amidala to rescue Obi-Wan Kenobi.

OUTCOME:
Anakin Skywalker and Padmé Amidala captured. MISSION FAILED.

2. EXECUTION ARENA

OBJECTIVE:
Anakin, Padmé, and Obi-Wan to escape execution.

OUTCOME:
Captives survive and destroy vicious beasts. MISSION COMPLETE.

3. JEDI STRIKE FORCE

OBJECTIVE:
Jedi team to rescue captives from droids.

OUTCOME:
Many Jedi killed, Jedi survivors surrounded by droid army. MISSION INCOMPLETE.

"Begun, the CLONE WARS have." Yoda

SEPARATISTS:

- BATTLE DROIDS
- SUPER BATTLE DROIDS
- SPIDER DROIDS
- DROIDEKAS
- WEAPONS: BLASTER RIFLES

REPUBLIC:
- JEDI
- CLONE TROOPERS
- AT-TE WALKERS
- LAAT/I GUNSHIPS
- WEAPONS: BLASTER RIFLES, LIGHTSABERS

4. ARRIVAL OF CLONE ARMY

OBJECTIVE:
Clone army to rescue survivors.

OUTCOME:
Survivors airlifted out of arena. MISSION COMPLETE.

5. DESERT BATTLE

OBJECTIVE:
Jedi to lead clone troopers and vehicles against droid army.

OUTCOME:
Despite many fatalities during a full-scale battle, clone army is victorious. MISSION COMPLETE.

6. DUEL WITH DOOKU

OBJECTIVE:
Obi-Wan, Anakin, and Yoda to prevent Count Dooku's escape from Geonosis.

OUTCOME:
Anakin loses his arm, Count Dooku escapes. MISSION FAILED.

CONSEQUENCES

The Battle of Geonosis concludes with heavy losses on both sides, including hundreds of Jedi. After a fierce duel, Count Dooku escapes with plans for a Death Star. Palpatine, as Supreme Chancellor, has taken control of the Republic as the Clone Wars begin.

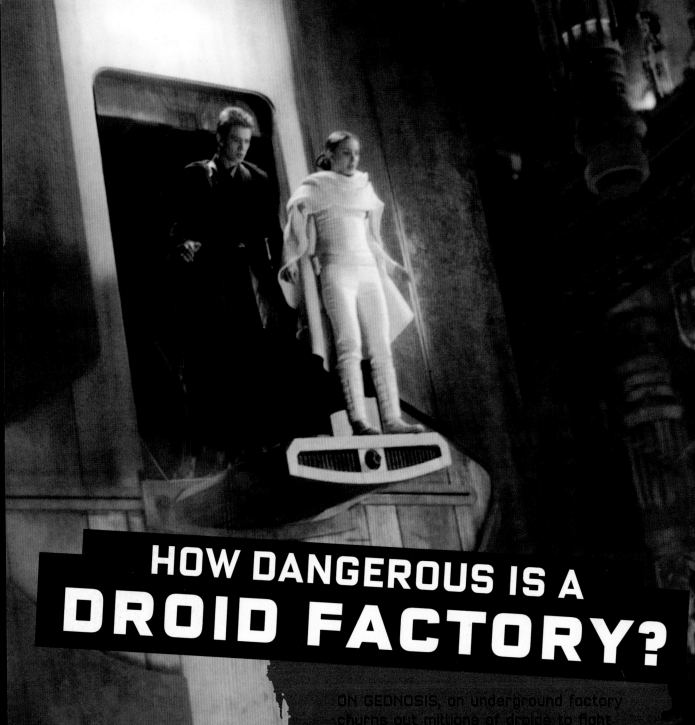

HOW DANGEROUS IS A
DROID FACTORY?

ON GEONOSIS, an underground factory churns out millions of droids to fight in Count Dooku's army. The machines run by themselves, and getting in their way can be deadly. Anakin, Padmé, and C-3PO get a close-up view when they are on the trail of Obi-Wan, who has been captured by the Separatists.

To the factory machine, there's no difference between battle droids and protocol droids. A blade knocks off C-3PO's head and welds it onto a new battle droid body. Luckily, C-3PO can survive losing his head, though the fretful droid finds it all very confusing.

Anakin fights Geonosian warriors on the moving belts until a machine clamps his right arm under a piece of metal! He eventually gets loose, but his lightsaber is ruined.

MISSION DATA

■ Battle droids are made by other droids, as humans are too easily injured. C-3PO is amazed at the huge operation: "Machines making machines!" he marvels.

Padmé is nearly covered in red-hot metal, but R2-D2 switches off the pouring machine just in time. Padmé is free, but she quickly discovers the most dangerous things in the droid factory are the Geonosians who guard it!

DC-15
BLASTER
RIFLE

Clone
ARMY

The Republic doesn't have a military unit of its own, so finding a ready-made army of clone fighters on Kamino seems too good to be true! As the Jedi Generals lead their new soldiers into battle against the Separatists, they don't realize that their troopers are secretly loyal to Darth Sidious.

The clone army is equipped with starfighters, tanks, speeders, and warships. On Coruscant, thousands of clones march into troop carriers on their way to fight the Separatists.

PHASE I ARMOR

ARMOR HAS
20 SEPARATE
PIECES

RESTRICTIVE ARMOR
The early clone troopers wore Phase I armor with its distinctive helmet fin and pure white color. Made of plastoid, the armor provided protection against explosions and shrapnel, but it wasn't very easy to move around in. It was soon replaced with Phase II armor.

CHAIN OF COMMAND
CHANCELLOR PALPATINE

JEDI GENERALS

CLONE COMMANDERS

CLONE CAPTAINS

CLONE LIEUTENANTS

CLONE SERGEANTS

CLONE TROOPERS

BORN TO FIGHT
Each clone is grown from the DNA of the bounty hunter Jango Fett. Clones are designed to age twice as fast as normal humans and are trained for a life of combat.

PHASE II ARMOR

DC-15A BLASTER FIRES 500 SHOTS FROM A SINGLE GAS CARTRIDGE

POUCHES CONTAIN MEDICAL KIT AND EXTRA AMMUNITION

ARMOR HAS SPECIAL ANTI-BLASTER COATING

ARMOR UPDATES
The Phase II armor is designed with improvements learned from battle experience. It is more comfortable, stands up to blaster fire, and comes in camouflage colors when required.

Clone Trooper
IDENTIFICATION

You can't win a war without adapting to changing circumstances. At the start of the Clone Wars, every trooper wore identical armor. But as the fighting spread to hundreds of planets, clone armor became customized to get the job done better. Color markings now denote unit affiliation, while extra equipment or design adjustments adapt the armor to suit the needs of individual missions.

CLONE TROOPER
Basic clone trooper armor is plain white and blaster resistant. However, it is not always suitable for working in extreme environments or handling specialized equipment.

CLONE COMMANDERS

COMMANDER NEYO
Leader of the 91st Reconnaissance Corps, Neyo is an expert BARC speeder pilot. His helmet has been adjusted so it is extra streamlined.

COMMANDER BLY
Bly serves with the Star Corps. The viewfinder on his helmet provides better visibility in the jungles of Felucia.

COMMANDER CODY
The troopers of the 212th Attack Battalion report to Cody, who stays in control with built-in radio antennas.

SHOCK TROOPER

Shock Troopers are members of the Coruscant Guard. They act as bodyguards for Chancellor Palpatine and other important officials, and are easily identifiable by the red markings on their armor.

CLONE PILOT

Pilots can fly everything from ARC-170s to V-wings. Their armor contains a life-support pack.

AT-RT DRIVER

AT-RT drivers wear camouflage armor and have a lifeform scanner attached to their gun strap.

COMMANDER GREE

Gree is an expert in alien cultures. When working with the Wookiees on the jungle planet Kashyyyk, he wears green camouflage armor.

GALACTIC MARINE

Members of the 21st Nova Corps, Marines are trained to fight in many environments, and their Synthmesh helmet screens keep out sand, dust, and grit.

ENVIRONMENT SPECIALISTS

COMMANDER BACARA

Bacara is one of the leaders of the Galactic Marines. He wears the maroon colors of the Marines, and a protective kama around his waist to indicate rank.

SWAMP TROOPER

With lightweight, camouflaged armor, swamp troopers can operate on soggy planets where heavy equipment would just sink into mud.

VEHICLES

THE REPUBLIC

During the Clone Wars, enormous Republic assault ships and cruisers transport thousands of Jedi and clone forces to battlefields across the galaxy. Walkers, tanks, starfighters, and gunships are commanded by clones on land, in the sky, and in space! The Jedi have powerful vessels, too; their ships are fast and nimble.

ALL TERRAIN TACTICAL ENFORCER (AT-TE)
- **SIZE** 22m (72 ft) LONG
- **SPEED** 60 km/hr (37 mph)
- **CAPACITY** 45 TROOPERS
- **WEAPONS** 6 ANTI-PERSONNEL CANNONS, 1 MASS-DRIVER CANNON

ALL TERRAIN OPEN TRANSPORT (AT-OT)
- **SIZE** 14.3 m (47 ft) LONG
- **SPEED** 55 km/hr (34 mph)
- **CAPACITY** 35 TROOPERS
- **WEAPONS** 4 LASER CANNONS

SWAMP SPEEDER
- **SIZE** 5 m (16.4 ft) LONG
- **SPEED** 100 km/hr (62 mph)
- **CAPACITY** 1 PILOT, 1 GUNNER
- **WEAPONS** 2 BLASTER CANNONS

CLONE TURBO TANK
- **SIZE** 49.4 m (162.1 ft) LONG
- **SPEED** 160 km/hr (99 mph)
- **CAPACITY** 300 TROOPERS
- **WEAPONS** 1 HEAVY LASER CANNON, 1 REPEATING LASER CANNON, 2 ANTI-PERSONNEL LASER CANNONS, 2 BLASTER CANNONS, 2 GRENADE LAUNCHERS

ALL TERRAIN ATTACK POD (AT-AP)
- **SIZE** 11 m (36.1 ft) TALL
- **SPEED** 60 km/hr (37 mph)
- **CAPACITY** 1 PILOT, 2 GUNNERS
- **WEAPONS** 1 HEAVY BLASTER CANNON, 1 MEDIUM BLASTER CANNON, 1 PROJECTILE LAUNCHER

ALL TERRAIN RECON TRANSPORT (AT-RT)
- **SIZE** 3.2 m (10.5 ft) TALL
- **SPEED** 75 km/hr (47 mph)
- **CAPACITY** 1 PILOT
- **WEAPONS** 1 LASER CANNON

LAND

TURBOLASER DESTROYS ESCAPING STARSHIPS

WEAPON CAN BE REPLACED WITH ION CANNON OR MISSILE LAUNCHER

CLONE COMMANDERS WATCH BATTLEFIELD AND GIVE ORDERS

THICK ARMOR

12 LEGS PROVIDE STABILITY

SELF-PROPELLED HEAVY ARTILLERY-TURBOLASER (SPHA-T)
- **SIZE** 140.2 m (460 ft) LONG
- **SPEED** 35 km/hr (22 mph)
- **CAPACITY** 15 CREW, 10 GUNNERS
- **WEAPONS** 1 TURBOLASER, 12 ANTI-PERSONNEL LASERS

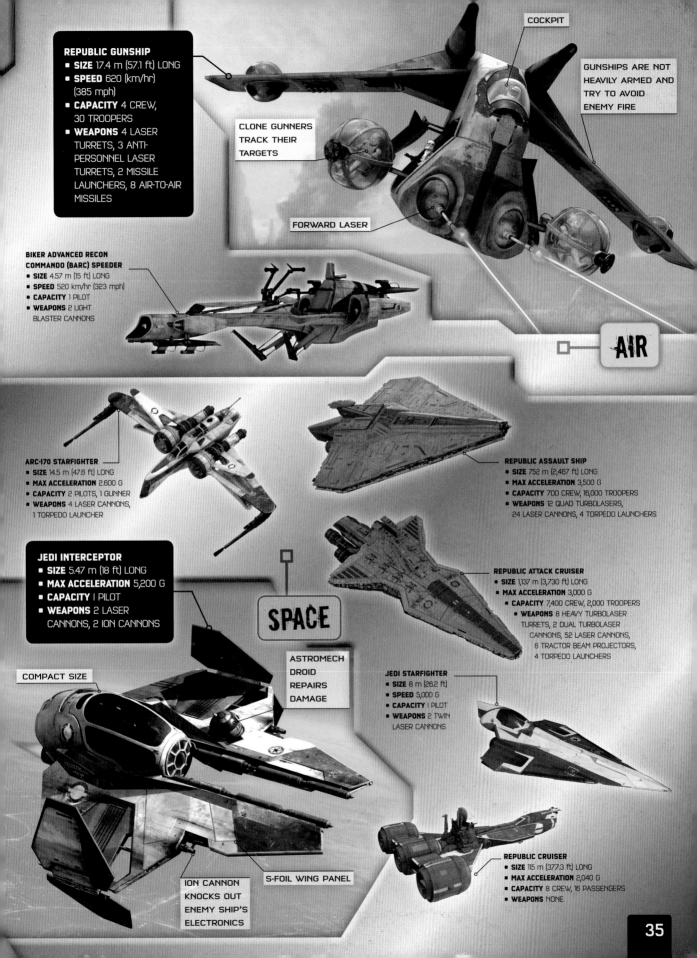

REPUBLIC GUNSHIP
- **SIZE** 17.4 m (57.1 ft) LONG
- **SPEED** 620 (km/hr) (385 mph)
- **CAPACITY** 4 CREW, 30 TROOPERS
- **WEAPONS** 4 LASER TURRETS, 3 ANTI-PERSONNEL LASER TURRETS, 2 MISSILE LAUNCHERS, 8 AIR-TO-AIR MISSILES

COCKPIT

GUNSHIPS ARE NOT HEAVILY ARMED AND TRY TO AVOID ENEMY FIRE

CLONE GUNNERS TRACK THEIR TARGETS

FORWARD LASER

BIKER ADVANCED RECON COMMANDO (BARC) SPEEDER
- **SIZE** 4.57 m (15 ft) LONG
- **SPEED** 520 km/hr (323 mph)
- **CAPACITY** 1 PILOT
- **WEAPONS** 2 LIGHT BLASTER CANNONS

AIR

ARC-170 STARFIGHTER
- **SIZE** 14.5 m (47.6 ft) LONG
- **MAX ACCELERATION** 2.600 G
- **CAPACITY** 2 PILOTS, 1 GUNNER
- **WEAPONS** 4 LASER CANNONS, 1 TORPEDO LAUNCHER

REPUBLIC ASSAULT SHIP
- **SIZE** 752 m (2,467 ft) LONG
- **MAX ACCELERATION** 3,500 G
- **CAPACITY** 700 CREW, 16,000 TROOPERS
- **WEAPONS** 12 QUAD TURBOLASERS, 24 LASER CANNONS, 4 TORPEDO LAUNCHERS

JEDI INTERCEPTOR
- **SIZE** 5.47 m (18 ft) LONG
- **MAX ACCELERATION** 5,200 G
- **CAPACITY** 1 PILOT
- **WEAPONS** 2 LASER CANNONS, 2 ION CANNONS

REPUBLIC ATTACK CRUISER
- **SIZE** 1,137 m (3,730 ft) LONG
- **MAX ACCELERATION** 3,000 G
- **CAPACITY** 7,400 CREW, 2,000 TROOPERS
- **WEAPONS** 8 HEAVY TURBOLASER TURRETS, 2 DUAL TURBOLASER CANNONS, 52 LASER CANNONS, 6 TRACTOR BEAM PROJECTORS, 4 TORPEDO LAUNCHERS

SPACE

ASTROMECH DROID REPAIRS DAMAGE

COMPACT SIZE

JEDI STARFIGHTER
- **SIZE** 8 m (26.2 ft)
- **SPEED** 5,000 G
- **CAPACITY** 1 PILOT
- **WEAPONS** 2 TWIN LASER CANNONS

ION CANNON KNOCKS OUT ENEMY SHIP'S ELECTRONICS

S-FOIL WING PANEL

REPUBLIC CRUISER
- **SIZE** 115 m (377.3 ft) LONG
- **MAX ACCELERATION** 2,040 G
- **CAPACITY** 8 CREW, 16 PASSENGERS
- **WEAPONS** NONE

WHAT HAPPENS WHEN DROIDS FIGHT CLONES?

AT THE BATTLE OF GEONOSIS, Count Dooku's droid army is huge, and the Republic's clone troopers are outnumbered and outgunned. However, they are smarter than their robot foes. It is the clone troopers' first fight—and they are ready!

■ The clone troopers have been training for nearly ten years. Their cloning center on Kamino has areas where the troopers practice military missions and strategy.

Clone troopers are living beings, who can outthink battle droids. Officers direct the battle from a clone command station, which means they take control of the battlefield. Some of the Trade Federation's ships try to escape but the clone troopers quickly shoot them down.

Droids follow each other without question. If one droid is destroyed, a dozen more can take its place. Clone troopers, however, can think for themselves and react to changing situations—a skill that saves lives and wins battles.

DARTH VADER

BETRAYED

Darth Tyranus used to be a Jedi called Count Dooku. He thinks he's more important than everyone else, but he doesn't realize that Darth Sidious is using him in order to gain a more powerful apprentice—until Darth Sidious orders Anakin to kill him.

Darth Sidious tempts Anakin Skywalker into joining the Sith so he can become more powerful. Consumed by the dark side, Anakin takes the name Darth Vader and attacks his former friends.

DARTH VADER WILL REPLACE ANAKIN'S LIGHTSABER WITH A RED-BLADED ONE

Sith LORDS

The Sith have been the enemies of the Jedi for thousands of years. They follow the dark side of the Force and thrive on anger, greed, and fear. They crave power above everything else and use war as a tool to weaken their enemies.

Mustafarian Blaster Rifle

Clone Trooper Blaster Rifle

Neimoidian Blaster Rifle

Utapaun Blaster Rifle

Coruscant Senate Guard Blaster Rifle

Geonosian Sonic Blaster Rifle

Boba Fett's Blaster Rifle

BLASTER RIFLES

These heavy blaster weapons must be carried with two hands, but they can fire further and more accurately than blaster pistols. Clone troopers and stormtroopers are never seen without blaster rifles on the battlefield.

Clone Trooper Blaster Rifle

Imperial Stormtrooper Blaster Rifle

_____ Blaster Rifle

Flash Speeder Gun

Electrostaff

Thermal Detonator

Naboo Laser Light

MISCELLANEOUS WEAPONS

Warriors need to adapt to their situation. Use a laser light to signal friends, and a saberdart to strike distant foes. Electrostaffs take out one enemy at a time, while thermal detonators can clear out an entire room.

Saberdart

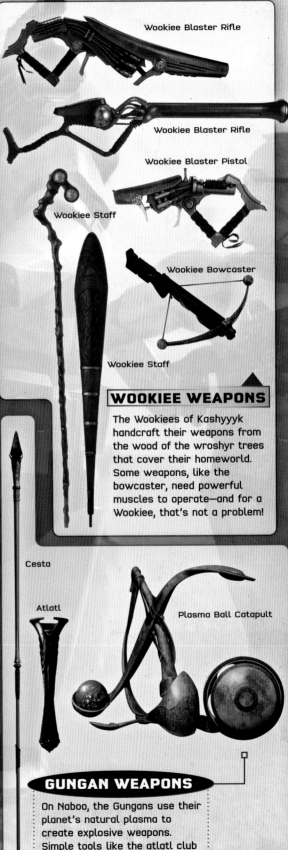

Wookiee Blaster Rifle

Wookiee Blaster Rifle

Wookiee Blaster Pistol

Wookiee Staff

Wookiee Bowcaster

Wookiee Staff

WOOKIEE WEAPONS

The Wookiees of Kashyyyk handcraft their weapons from the wood of the wroshyr trees that cover their homeworld. Some weapons, like the bowcaster, need powerful muscles to operate—and for a Wookiee, that's not a problem!

Cesta

Atlatl

Plasma Ball Catapult

GUNGAN WEAPONS

On Naboo, the Gungans use their planet's natural plasma to create explosive weapons. Simple tools like the atlatl club and the long-handled cesta can throw powerful plasma energy balls great distances.

CORUSCANT

PLANET: Coruscant
LOCATION: Core worlds
TERRAIN: One single gigantic city, including the seat of the Republic's government
INHABITANTS: Humans plus many different alien species
ALLEGIANCE: Republic

With the Clone Wars in full swing, Separatist warships surround the Republic capital of Coruscant. Their plot is not conquest—it's kidnapping! Chancellor Palpatine is a prisoner aboard General Grievous's command ship, *Invisible Hand*. It's up to Obi-Wan Kenobi and Anakin Skywalker to rescue the Republic ruler. If they can eliminate some of the Separatist commanders along the way, they might help the Republic make progress in the Clone Wars.

1. INVISIBLE HAND

OBJECTIVE:
Anakin and Obi-Wan to fight their way to Grievous's flagship.

OUTCOME:
The Jedi defeat droids and land successfully on *Invisible Hand*. MISSION COMPLETE.

BATTLE STATS

SEPARATISTS:
- BUZZ DROIDS
- BATTLE DROIDS
- VULTURE DROIDS
- MAGNAGUARDS
- WEAPONS: ELECTROSTAFFS, LIGHTSABERS, BLASTERS

REPUBLIC:
- ARC-170 STARFIGHTERS
- ETA-2 INTERCEPTORS
- REPUBLIC ATTACK CRUISERS
- CLONE TROOPERS
- WEAPONS: LIGHTSABERS, BLASTERS

2. PALPATINE

OBJECTIVE:
Jedi to find the Chancellor aboard the huge ship.

OUTCOME:
Palpatine is located with help from R2-D2. MISSION COMPLETE.

"Time to abandon SHIP!"

3. SITH DUEL

OBJECTIVE:
Anakin and Obi-Wan to capture Count Dooku.

OUTCOME:
Count Dooku defeated and killed by Anakin. MISSION INCOMPLETE.

4. ESCAPE

OBJECTIVE:
Rescue party to get off the flagship before it's destroyed by the Republic fleet.

OUTCOME:
Rescue party is captured. Republic attack damages the ship. MISSION FAILED.

5. GENERAL GRIEVOUS

OBJECTIVE:
Jedi to eliminate General Grievous, leader of the Separatist army.

OUTCOME:
Grievous's MagnaGuards are destroyed, but the general escapes. MISSION FAILED.

6. ROCKY LANDING

OBJECTIVE:
Anakin to land the damaged *Invisible Hand*.

OUTCOME:
Anakin steers the ship to a safe landing on Coruscant; Palpatine is safe. MISSION COMPLETE.

CONSEQUENCES

Following the Battle of Coruscant, the Separatists have lost both their flagship and their leader, Count Dooku. With General Grievous still on the loose, however, the Clone Wars are far from over. And Anakin will soon learn that Chancellor Palpatine is a Sith Lord who hopes to make him his apprentice.

WHAT USE IS ONE SMALL ASTROMECH DROID?

ASTROMECH DROIDS may not look like much, but they are proof that good things come in small packages! Anakin's droid, R2-D2, is good at getting himself and his friends out of trouble. During the Battle of Coruscant, he proves he is both smart and brave when he helps Anakin and Obi-Wan rescue Chancellor Palpatine. He also saves himself from super battle droids by starting a big oil fire.

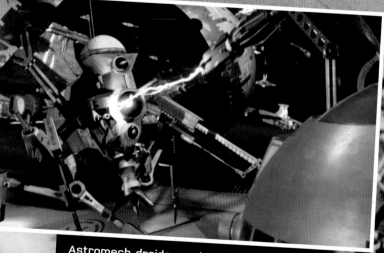

Astromech droids are built to help fly and fix starships, but they can do so much more. Above Coruscant, R2-D2 is perfectly positioned on the wing of Anakin's starship to zap an attacking buzz droid.

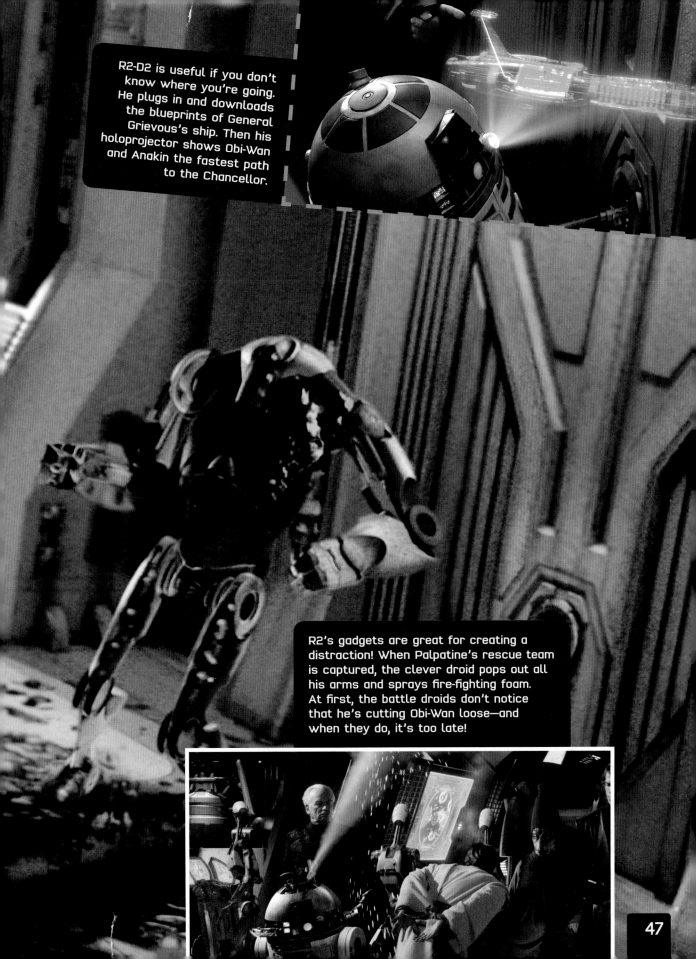

R2-D2 is useful if you don't know where you're going. He plugs in and downloads the blueprints of General Grievous's ship. Then his holoprojector shows Obi-Wan and Anakin the fastest path to the Chancellor.

R2's gadgets are great for creating a distraction! When Palpatine's rescue team is captured, the clever droid pops out all his arms and sprays fire-fighting foam. At first, the battle droids don't notice that he's cutting Obi-Wan loose—and when they do, it's too late!

HOW CAN A JEDI FIGHT WITHOUT A LIGHTSABER?

OBI-WAN KENOBI IS in trouble. He's been sent to Utapau to defeat Separatist cyborg General Grievous, but he drops his lightsaber during a bumpy ride on Boga, his varactyl steed. Grievous and his MagnaGuards are a threatening sight —are they too much for a Jedi with no lightsaber? Obi-Wan really needs to think of a way out of this one. Fast.

Obi-Wan isn't intimidated easily. Grievous might have a super-fast wheel bike, but Obi-Wan jumps onto Boga, who keeps up just fine. Obi-Wan grabs Grievous's electrostaff and attacks him with it, leaping onto the speeding bike.

Obi-Wan has enough Jedi wisdom to realize that a weapon is only as good as whoever holds it. Even though he thinks blasters are "uncivilized," Obi-Wan channels his Jedi skill into getting a clean shot at Grievous, and succeeds in destroying the villain.

49

DECOYS AND *Disguise*

Charging into danger with blasters blazing is sometimes a guaranteed way to lose! Going undercover can be tricky, but it might be the best way to uncover carefully guarded secrets. Disguises can also come in handy when protecting important people from their enemies. If you need to don a sneaky disguise, here are some tried and tested tips.

2. BE INCONSPICUOUS

Stranded on Tatooine, Qui-Gon Jinn tries to blend in to avoid trouble. He conceals his lightsaber and Jedi clothing while he searches for a new hyperdrive for Queen Amidala's ship.

1. MIX IT UP

Queen Amidala of Naboo has many handmaidens. They are great bodyguards, but that's not all: They look so much like the Queen that any of them can take her place. When a handmaiden puts on the Queen's clothing and makeup, Amidala becomes a red-robed handmaiden. No one knows that the "Queen" is a decoy!

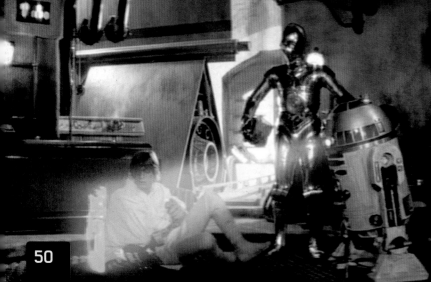

3. USE A DROID

Droids make excellent spies— as well as great hiding places! An astromech droid like R2-D2 can download and carry lots of information, and droids are so common that most people ignore them. R2 escapes with Princess Leia's message because the Imperials are too busy scanning for lifeforms to notice a droid.

4. BORROW A UNIFORM

Disguising yourself as a member of the enemy is almost always a good plan, especially if they wear armor and helmets that will help hide your identity. Aboard the Death Star, Luke Skywalker and Han Solo change into stormtrooper armor and walk straight into the detention center.

5. BE SNEAKY

Sometimes the best plans take shape at the last minute. Han Solo poses as an AT-ST driver when the Rebels can't get into the Empire's shield bunker. His gamble pays off when the back door is opened!

7. HIDE IN PLAIN SIGHT

Not even the Jedi realized that Chancellor Palpatine, ruler of the Republic, was really the Sith Lord Darth Sidious. By acting like he had nothing to hide, he hid the biggest secret of all. If you go undercover, make sure you keep calm and act confident at all times.

6. REALLY MEAN IT

Sometimes you need to go deep undercover. To infiltrate the heart of your enemy's stronghold, you must truly act the part. When Princess Leia poses as the bounty hunter Boushh, she plays the role of a tough criminal by threatening Jabba with a thermal detonator!

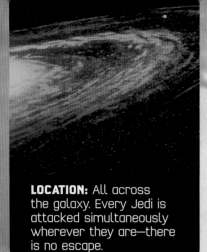

JEDI PURGE

LOCATION: All across the galaxy. Every Jedi is attacked simultaneously wherever they are—there is no escape.

Darth Sidious has been planning to destroy the Jedi for years, and as the Clone Wars come to an end he springs his trap! Because Sidious is also Chancellor Palpatine, the leader of the Republic, the clone troopers of the Republic army must obey his commands—they have been brainwashed to do so. He issues Order 66, which states that all Jedi are traitors to the Republic, and across the galaxy the troopers turn on their Jedi Generals and friends.

1. THE ORDER

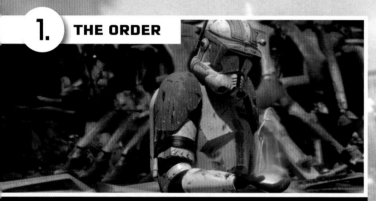

OBJECTIVE:
Darth Sidious to activate Order 66 via hologram.

OUTCOME:
Across the galaxy, clone commanders receive the deadly instruction. MISSION COMPLETE.

2. UTAPAU

OBJECTIVE:
Clones to destroy all Jedi on Utapau.

OUTCOME:
Clones fire at Obi-Wan. He falls into a crater, but survives. MISSION FAILED.

3. MYGEETO

OBJECTIVE:
Clones to destroy all Jedi on Mygeeto.

OUTCOME:
Ki-Adi-Mundi is felled by his troops. MISSION COMPLETE.

4. FELUCIA

OBJECTIVE:
Clones to destroy all Jedi on Felucia.

OUTCOME:
Aayla Secura is shot in the back by her own soldiers. MISSION COMPLETE.

BATTLE STATS

CLONE ARMY:

- SITH
- CLONE TROOPERS
- BARC SPEEDERS
- ARC-170 STARFIGHTERS
- TURBO TANKS
- WEAPONS: BLASTERS

JEDI:

- JEDI
- DELTA-7 STARFIGHTERS
- 74-Z SPEEDERS
- WEAPONS: LIGHTSABERS

"The time has come. Execute ORDER 66."

Darth Sidious

5. KASHYYYK

OBJECTIVE:
Clones to destroy all Jedi on Kashyyyk.

OUTCOME:
Yoda senses danger. He fights the clones and escapes.
MISSION FAILED.

6. SALEUCAMI

OBJECTIVE:
Clones to destroy all Jedi on Saleucami.

OUTCOME:
Clones blow up Stass Allie's speeder bike.
MISSION COMPLETE.

7. CATO NEIMOIDIA

OBJECTIVE:
Clones to destroy all Jedi on Cato Neimoidia.

OUTCOME:
Clone pilots destroy Plo Koon's Jedi starfighter.
MISSION COMPLETE.

CONSEQUENCES

The Jedi Purge leaves the Jedi Order defeated and the surviving Jedi are too few to stop Darth Sidious. The Sith Lord seizes control of the galaxy and names himself Emperor. After thousands of years of Jedi power, their fire has gone out of the universe. Dark days follow.

8. CORUSCANT

OBJECTIVE:
Darth Vader to wipe out all Jedi in the Jedi Temple.

OUTCOME:
Vader and a squad of clones massacre all the Jedi.
MISSION COMPLETE.

MIGHTY WARRIOR

Tarfful is one of Chewbacca's oldest friends. When Kashyyyk is attacked, he steps up to defend his homeland. Taking charge of the defenses for Kachirho City, Tarfful is ready to show the droid army that the Wookiees are the best fighters in the galaxy.

SOME WOOKIEES HAVE HUNDREDS OF YEARS OF BATTLE EXPERIENCE

TARFFUL

ARMOR PLATING DEFLECTS BLASTER FIRE

CHEWBACCA

CHEWBACCA IS A GOOD PILOT AND MECHANIC

FORMIDABLE FORCE

Wookiees on the warpath have been known to pull people's arms from their sockets! They are nearly unstoppable when enraged, but always obey their city's war chieftain, Tarfful. During the Battle of Kashyyyk, Wookiees and clone troopers fight side by side.

54

WOOKIEE STATS

LEADER: KING GRAKCHAWWAA

ALLEGIANCE: REPUBLIC

HEADQUARTERS: KASHYYYK

WEAPONS: BOWCASTER, BLASTER, SLUG THROWER

VEHICLES: ORNITHOPTER, FLYING CATAMARAN

VALUES: SOCIETY, LOYALTY

FLUTTERING INTO ACTION
The Wookiee ornithopter is a lightweight flyer used for scouting. Like all Wookiee creations it is hand-crafted from local materials, unlike the factory-made war machines of the Separatists.

WOOKIEE BOWCASTER FIRES ENERGY BULLETS

HAIRY HERO
Loyal and brave, Chewbacca puts his bowcaster to good use during the Battle of Kashyyyk. He survives to fight another day and later battles against the Empire with his friend, Han Solo.

Wookiees have deep family bonds and prefer to stay on their home planet, Kashyyyk. With help from Yoda and the Republic's clone troopers, they push back the invading battle droids.

Wookiee ARMY

Wookiees may be strong and fierce, but they are also friendly creatures who live in harmony with nature. When the Separatists invade the planet Kashyyyk, they quickly learn that there's hardly anything more dangerous than an angry Wookiee!

CHAIN OF COMMAND

KING GRAKCHAWWAA

CITY WAR CHIEFTAIN TARFFUL

WOOKIEE WARRIORS

Clone Trooper to STORMTROOPER

The helmet has a T-shaped visor that closely resembles the one worn by Jango Fett. It also has a fin on top.

The Clone Wars are over. The Republic is now an oppressive Empire and Chancellor Palpatine has taken control as Emperor. And he doesn't have to look far to find an army to do his bidding. With only a few modifications, the Republic's clone troopers are swiftly transformed into Imperial stormtroopers. Their mission may have changed from defeating Separatists to destroying Rebels, but these troopers have always stayed loyal to their commander.

Each trooper carries a standard issue DC-15A blaster rifle which can fire up to 500 shots on a single ammo pack.

JANGO FETT

This deadly bounty hunter caught the attention of Count Dooku, who hired him to be the source of the genetic material used to create the clones. Jango also helped train the clones, and their armor —especially the Phase I design— is clearly based on Jango's Mandalorian battle armor.

ORIGINS OF THE CLONE

Rocket backpack also contains a missile

Gauntlet can spray fire at enemies

Phase I armor is made up of a black bodysuit, surrounded by a 20-piece blaster-resistant shell. Commanders have yellow markings.

PHASE I CLONE TROOPER

Early clone troopers wear identical white armor—except for commanders, who have colored markings. This armor is bulky and uncomfortable for long-term combat.

The new helmet includes an advanced air filtration system, while the visor contains a targeting system and screen that displays important information.

The helmet is now fully sealed and can supply emergency air for 20 minutes. Some troopers complain about the smaller eyeholes.

The DC-15A blaster rifle is still in use, but troopers also carry special weapons if needed.

Stormtroopers carry the E-11 blaster rifle. On its automatic setting, it fires blaster bolts at an extremely high rate of speed.

This armor can survive explosions and blaster hits, and the foot casing can be magnetized. Phase II armor is easily personalized to denote unit affiliation, or painted in camouflage colors.

Stormtrooper armor consists of only 18 blaster-resistant pieces, surrounding a black bodysuit that can adapt to extreme temperatures.

PHASE II CLONE TROOPER

Battlefield experience in the Clone Wars leads to Phase II armor. It is more flexible and comfortable. Troopers often adapt or paint their armor for particular missions.

IMPERIAL STORMTROOPER

To symbolize the purity of the new Empire, stormtrooper armor returns to the all-white coloration of the earliest clones. The look inspires fear across the galaxy!

IMPERIAL ARMY STATS

LEADER: EMPEROR PALPATINE
ALLEGIANCE: EMPIRE
HEADQUARTERS: CORUSCANT
WEAPONS: E-11 BLASTER RIFLE, THERMAL DETONATOR, E-WEB HEAVY REPEATING BLASTER
VEHICLES: AT-AT, AT-ST, TIE FIGHTER, TIE INTERCEPTOR, TIE BOMBER, STAR DESTROYER
VALUES: OBEDIENCE, DESTROYING ALL ENEMIES

REVIEWING THE TROOPS

As the Emperor's right-hand man, Darth Vader outranks most officers. The Sith Lord has the power to command legions of stormtroopers and has his own ship—the Super Star Destroyer—*Executor*.

Stormtroopers are a special branch of the Imperial forces, and most of them are clones. The Imperial military also includes army and navy troopers, TIE fighter pilots, AT-AT drivers, and the Emperor's red-robed Royal Guard.

Imperial ARMY

The Empire has one of the most powerful militaries in the history of the galaxy. Well-equipped and well-trained, there are thousands of stormtroopers, starships, and vehicles ready to invade troublesome planets. The Imperial Army is confident it will crush the Rebellion, soon.

CHAIN OF COMMAND

EMPEROR PALPATINE

GRAND MOFFS

GENERALS/ADMIRALS

IMPERIAL OFFICERS

STORMTROOPERS

CLONE TO STORM

Clone troopers became stormtroopers when the Clone Wars ended with Order 66. Specialty units such as snowtroopers, sandtroopers, and scout troopers are easily recognized by distinctive armor.

IMPERIAL STORMTROOPER

HELMET CONTAINS TARGETING EQUIPMENT

INSIGNIA SHOWS HIGH RANK

GRAND MOFF TARKIN

SUPERIOR

Grand Moff Tarkin is in charge of the Death Star project and has served the Emperor since the beginning. Cruel and power-hungry, he is one of the few Imperial officials with enough authority to give orders to Darth Vader!

REPUBLIC FIGHTER

The ARC-170 is a heavy starfighter often used as a bomber. It only takes an ARC-170, two pilots, a gunner, and an astromech droid to make enemies turn and run!

ASSAULT SHIPS

Some starfighters can do everything from bombing to dogfighting. Certain features of the Republic's ARC-170 were incorporated into the Rebel Alliance's famous X-wing.

REBEL FAVORITE

The X-wing is a sturdy one-pilot ship, but it still uses an astromech. It offers a good balance of speed and firepower, and is equipped with two proton torpedoes.

WARTIME TRANSFORMATION

War can destroy, but it can also create. In order to gain an edge over their enemies, armies invent new technologies and designs to improve their starships and ground vehicles. Between the final days of the Republic and the fall of the Empire, the vehicles of combat became better and better, even though their basic shapes remained the same.

REPUBLIC MACHINE

This six-legged AT-TE walker is difficult to knock over and can even climb up cliff faces. It is packed with weapons, but can be destroyed by enemy cannons.

HEAVY WALKERS

Clone troopers used walkers to smash Separatist tanks during the Clone Wars. The design worked so well that the Empire built its own deadly walkers.

IMPERIAL MONSTER

The fearsome AT-AT towers over other war machines. It is less stable than the AT-TE but much tougher and scarier.

REPUBLIC SCOUT

The AT-RT is a small scouting vehicle that gives its driver a high vantage point to scan the territory, but it also makes him an easy target.

SCOUT WALKERS

The Republic army used two-legged walkers for fast scouting of unfamiliar terrain. The Imperial Army improved the design by adding more protection for the walker's drivers.

IMPERIAL THREAT

The Imperial AT-ST is taller than the AT-RT and its cockpit is completely enclosed. It is better armed as well, so keep clear—for your own safety!

REPUBLIC STAR

The Jedi Interceptor carries an astromech droid and is so small and maneuverable that it's hard to hit! Due to its compact size, it needs a hyperspace ring for long-distance travel.

INTERCEPTORS

The Jedi Interceptor was small, lightweight, and fast. Some parts of its design were used in Imperial TIE fighters, while others were incorporated into the Rebel Alliance's trusty A-wing.

REBEL SPEEDSTER

The A-wing doesn't have an astromech droid, but it does have a built-in hyperdrive engine for quick escapes. Rebel pilots love its speed!

REPUBLIC POWER

The Republic Attack Cruiser carries starfighters, walkers, and up to 2,000 soldiers. It can land directly on planets to unload its troops while giving covering fire.

DESTROYERS

In the Clone Wars, these huge ships carried clone troops. After installing more weapons, the Empire used Star Destroyers to smash Rebel battleships and conquer entire planets.

IMPERIAL MIGHT

The Imperial Star Destroyer is bigger than the Attack Cruiser and can't land on planets. But it can destroy targets from space with its turbolasers—and it carries squadrons of TIE fighters.

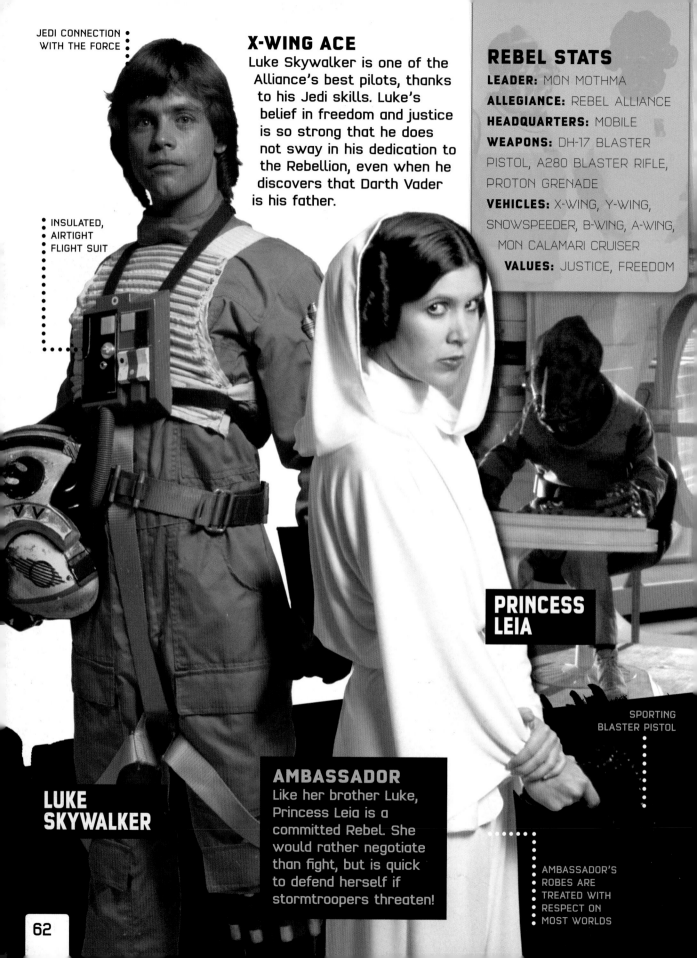

X-WING ACE

Luke Skywalker is one of the Alliance's best pilots, thanks to his Jedi skills. Luke's belief in freedom and justice is so strong that he does not sway in his dedication to the Rebellion, even when he discovers that Darth Vader is his father.

JEDI CONNECTION WITH THE FORCE

INSULATED, AIRTIGHT FLIGHT SUIT

REBEL STATS

LEADER: MON MOTHMA
ALLEGIANCE: REBEL ALLIANCE
HEADQUARTERS: MOBILE
WEAPONS: DH-17 BLASTER PISTOL, A280 BLASTER RIFLE, PROTON GRENADE
VEHICLES: X-WING, Y-WING, SNOWSPEEDER, B-WING, A-WING, MON CALAMARI CRUISER
VALUES: JUSTICE, FREEDOM

PRINCESS LEIA

LUKE SKYWALKER

AMBASSADOR

Like her brother Luke, Princess Leia is a committed Rebel. She would rather negotiate than fight, but is quick to defend herself if stormtroopers threaten!

SPORTING BLASTER PISTOL

AMBASSADOR'S ROBES ARE TREATED WITH RESPECT ON MOST WORLDS

ALLIANCE LEADERS

Mon Mothma, the senator from Chandrila, commands all the Rebel forces. Before each mission she meets with her Generals and Admirals to get their advice.

ADMIRAL ACKBAR

The navy is the backbone of the Rebel military. Admiral Ackbar and his people, the Mon Calamari, supply huge warships that can stand up to Imperial Star Destroyers. Ackbar is a brilliant commander who doesn't like to take foolish risks.

Rebel
ALLIANCE

The brave soldiers of the Rebel Alliance join together to defeat the Empire or die trying! Based in secret hideouts and using patched-together equipment, these hopeful volunteers must stay one step ahead of Darth Vader and the mighty Imperial military.

THE REBELS

The Rebels have to make do with whatever vehicles they can get, even when they're as unreliable as the *Millennium Falcon* can be! But, like the *Falcon*, Rebel ships pack a powerful punch. Ace pilots love the speedy X-wing and other starfighters, while big ships like Mon Calamari Cruisers can stand up to powerful Imperial Star Destroyers.

B-WING
- **SIZE** 16.9 m (55.4 ft) TALL
- **MAX ACCELERATION** 2,390 G
- **CAPACITY** 1 PILOT (PLUS 1 GUNNER IN SPECIAL MODELS)
- **WEAPONS** 3 ION CANNONS, 1 HEAVY LASER CANNON, 1 TWIN BLASTER, 2 TORPEDO LAUNCHERS

A-WING
- **SIZE** 9.6 m (31.5 ft) LONG
- **MAX ACCELERATION** 5,100 G
- **CAPACITY** 1 PILOT
- **WEAPONS** 2 LASER CANNONS, 2 MISSILE LAUNCHERS

NEBULON-B FRIGATE
- **SIZE** 300 m (984 ft) LONG
- **MAX ACCELERATION** 1,200 G
- **CAPACITY** 920 CREW, 75 PASSENGERS
- **WEAPONS** 12 TURBOLASERS, 12 LASER CANNONS, 2 TRACTOR BEAM PROJECTORS

SPACE

REBEL TRANSPORT
- **SIZE** 90 m (295 ft) LONG
- **MAX ACCELERATION** 900 G
- **CAPACITY** 7 CREW, 90 PASSENGERS
- **WEAPONS** 4 TWIN LASER TURRETS

Y-WING
- **SIZE** 16 m (52.5 ft) LONG
- **MAX ACCELERATION** 2,700 G
- **CAPACITY** 1 PILOT (PLUS 1 GUNNER IN SPECIAL MODELS)
- **WEAPONS** 2 LASER CANNONS, 2 ION CANNONS, 2 TORPEDO LAUNCHERS, PROTON BOMB

MON CALAMARI CRUISER
- **SIZE** 1,200 m (3,937 ft) LONG
- **MAX ACCELERATION** 2,750 G
- **CAPACITY** 5,400 CREW, 1,200 TROOPERS
- **WEAPONS** 48 TURBOLASERS, 20 ION CANNONS, 6 TRACTOR BEAM PROJECTORS

REBEL BLOCKADE RUNNER
- **SIZE** 150 m (492 ft) LONG
- **MAX ACCELERATION** 2,100 G
- **CAPACITY** 100 CREW, 600 PASSENGERS
- **WEAPONS** 2 TWIN TURBOLASERS, 4 SINGLE TURBOLASERS

MILLENNIUM FALCON
- **SIZE** 34.75 m (114 ft) LONG
- **MAX ACCELERATION** 3,000 G
- **CAPACITY** 2 PILOTS, 2 GUNNERS
- **WEAPONS** 2 QUAD LASER CANNONS, 1 CONCEALED BLASTER CANNON, 2 MISSILE LAUNCHERS

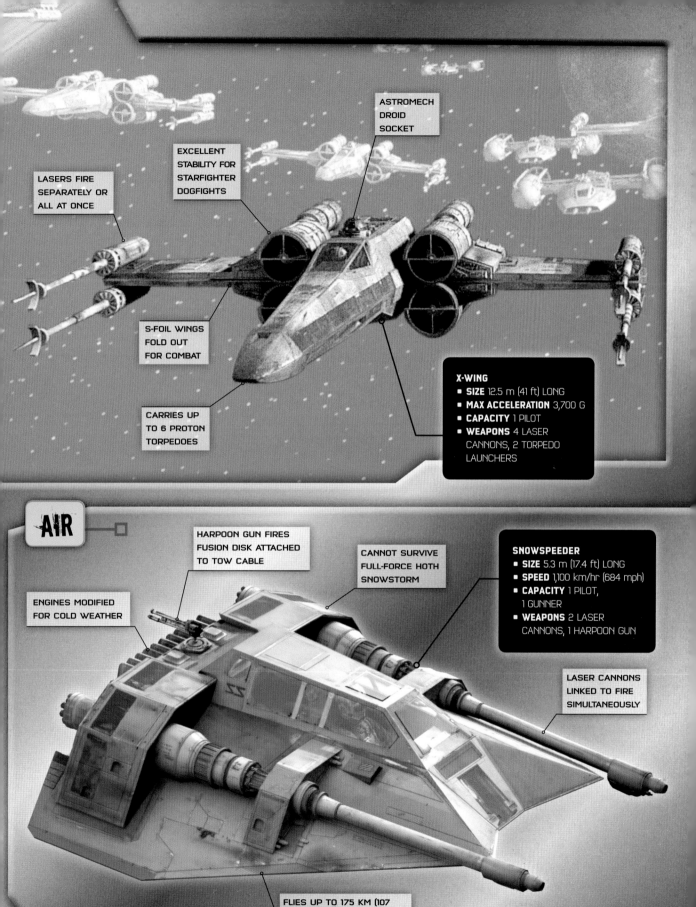

LASERS FIRE
SEPARATELY OR
ALL AT ONCE

EXCELLENT
STABILITY FOR
STARFIGHTER
DOGFIGHTS

ASTROMECH
DROID
SOCKET

S-FOIL WINGS
FOLD OUT
FOR COMBAT

CARRIES UP
TO 6 PROTON
TORPEDOES

X-WING
- **SIZE** 12.5 m (41 ft) LONG
- **MAX ACCELERATION** 3,700 G
- **CAPACITY** 1 PILOT
- **WEAPONS** 4 LASER
  CANNONS, 2 TORPEDO
  LAUNCHERS

AIR

HARPOON GUN FIRES
FUSION DISK ATTACHED
TO TOW CABLE

CANNOT SURVIVE
FULL-FORCE HOTH
SNOWSTORM

ENGINES MODIFIED
FOR COLD WEATHER

SNOWSPEEDER
- **SIZE** 5.3 m (17.4 ft) LONG
- **SPEED** 1,100 km/hr (684 mph)
- **CAPACITY** 1 PILOT,
  1 GUNNER
- **WEAPONS** 2 LASER
  CANNONS, 1 HARPOON GUN

LASER CANNONS
LINKED TO FIRE
SIMULTANEOUSLY

FLIES UP TO 175 KM (107
MILES) ABOVE GROUND

TARGET: THE
DEATH STAR

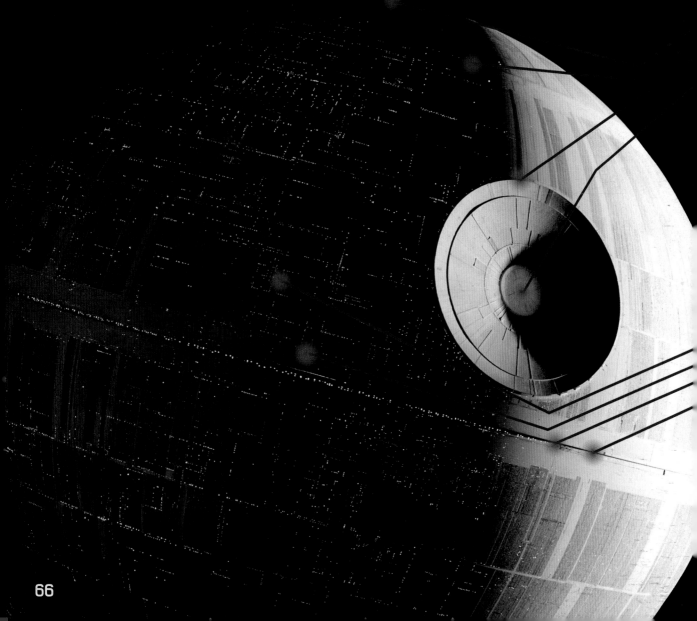

Rebel soldiers, it is time for action! But before going into battle, you must study your target. The Death Star is the biggest Imperial battle station ever built, and each part has a different function. Study the Death Star plans we have captured from our enemies so you can sneak into the Empire's base to rescue prisoners—or even destroy it from within.

Do not be fooled by a battle station that looks incomplete. The second Imperial Death Star might be fully operational, despite its appearance.

Decisions concerning Imperial warfare are made inside conference rooms like this one. Generals, Admirals, and Grand Moffs are some of the most important people in the Empire's upper ranks.

...ny Death Star systems ar... ...droids instead of humans. A sma... Rebel droid could locate the control room, plug into the Imperial computer bank, and access top-secret data.

...eath Star is so impo... ...tains a grand throne room... Emperor, should he choose to... The throne room sits in a tow... at the station's north pole.

The Death Star's powerful superlaser combines several energy beams into a single blast that smashes planets to smithereens.

Docking bays at the Death Star's equator hold TIE fighters and captured freighters. The bay is open to space and a magnetic force-field holds the air inside.

If they survive capture, Rebels might be held prisoner in one of the Death Star's detention bays. The jail cells are cold and uncomfortable—and supposedly escape-proof.

During a starfighter attack against the Death Star, you will need to watch out for the station's turbolasers. Hopefully the Rebel fighters will be too small for the targeting systems a...

Empty shafts lead down in the direction of the Death Star's reactor core. Tractor beam controls and other systems can be hard to reach, so watch your step!

"FEAR WILL KEEP THE LOCAL SYSTEMS IN LINE. FEAR OF THIS BATTLE STATION." GRAND MOFF TARKIN

HOW CAN A PRINCESS RESCUE HERSELF?

PRINCESS LEIA ISN'T afraid of anything. She is determined to bring down the Empire and her bold, fearless actions sometimes get her into trouble. But this is one princess who doesn't sit around waiting to be rescued. Leia's take-charge attitude usually saves her—and others.

Luke, Han, and Chewie free Leia from the Death Star's jail, but the princess quickly takes command. Picking up a stormtrooper's blaster, she clears a path to freedom.

Jabba the Hutt is the galaxy's worst gangster, and chaining Princess Leia to his throne is his last mistake. Leia uses the chain as a weapon to bring Jabba's evil rule to an end.

MISSION DATA

■ Princess Leia is the daughter of Anakin Skywalker and is strong in the Force. Although she hasn't been trained as a Jedi, she is a tough fighter and a smart negotiator.

PLANET: Yavin 4

LOCATION: Outer Rim Territories

TERRAIN: Jungle, ancient ruins, Rebel headquarters

INHABITANTS: Rebel Alliance soldiers

ALLEGIANCE: Rebel Alliance

The Emperor's Death Star has tracked the Rebels to their headquarters on the jungle moon of Yavin 4. The battle station's superlaser can blast the moon to rubble and will be ready to fire in only minutes. The Rebels have only one chance: If a starfighter can evade TIE fighters and hit the Death Star's tiny exhaust port, the station will explode. As the Rebel pilots board their ships, they know that they will either triumph—or die!

1. DEATH STAR APPROACH

OBJECTIVE:
Red and Gold Squadrons to weaken the Death Star's defences.

OUTCOME:
The Death Star's ion cannons and communications centers are taken out. MISSION COMPLETE.

2. SPACE BATTLE

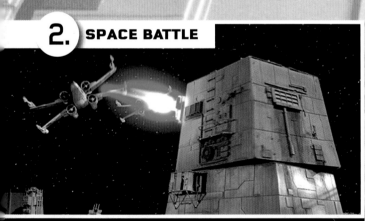

OBJECTIVE:
Rebel pilots to wipe out Imperial TIE fighters.

OUTCOME:
During fast-paced combat both sides take losses. MISSION FAILED.

BATTLE STATS

EMPIRE:
- SITH
- IMPERIAL TROOPS AND STAFF
- DEATH STAR
- TIE FIGHTERS
- TIE ADVANCED X1

REBEL ALLIANCE:

- STAR PILOTS
- T-65 X-WINGS
- BTL Y-WINGS
- *MILLENNIUM FALCON*

> ## "Great shot, kid, that was one in a million!"
>
> Han Solo to Luke Skywalker

3. FIRST TRENCH RUN

OBJECTIVE:
Gold Squadron's Y-wings to hit the Death Star's thermal exhaust port.

OUTCOME:
Y-wings destroyed by Darth Vader. MISSION FAILED.

4. SECOND TRENCH RUN

OBJECTIVE:
Red Squadron's X-wings to hit the thermal exhaust port.

OUTCOME:
X-wings fire but miss, and are destroyed by Darth Vader. MISSION FAILED.

5. DARTH VADER

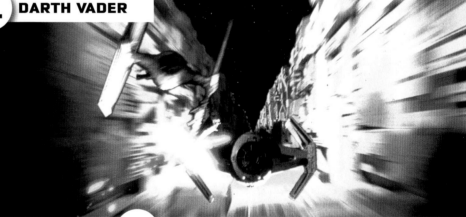

OBJECTIVE:
Millennium Falcon to attack Darth Vader.

OUTCOME:
Han Solo damages Vader's TIE fighter, allowing Luke to fire. MISSION COMPLETE.

6. FINAL CHANCE

CONSEQUENCES

The Battle of Yavin is a triumph for the Rebel Alliance, but they know that the Empire will soon strike back. The Rebels leave Yavin behind and build a new secret base on the frozen planet of Hoth. Luke Skywalker and Han Solo receive medals for their heroism and stay to help the Rebels in their fight.

OBJECTIVE:
Luke Skywalker to destroy the Death Star.

OUTCOME:
Luke uses the Force to strike the exhaust port, and blows up the Death Star. MISSION COMPLETE.

Obi-Wan Kenobi might be gone, but his spirit lives on in the Force. Luke uses his connection with the Force to hear Obi-Wan's advice. He turns off his targeting computer and trusts his instincts.

WHAT IS THE POWER OF THE FORCE?

THE FORCE IS A mystical energy field, and both the Jedi and the Sith can tap into it. It is extremely powerful and, if you know how to channel it, you can change the course of an entire battle. At the Battle of Yavin, both Luke Skywalker and Darth Vader use the Force to sharpen their focus and skill at high-speed piloting. But who will triumph in the end?

Luke calls on the Force to help guide his shot to the small target, and the proton torpedoes score a direct hit! The Death Star explodes, and as Luke flies away he hears Obi-Wan's voice: "The Force will be with you, always."

THE EMPIRE

The Empire's starships and vehicles are designed to make enemies run in terror! The mighty AT-AT walker shakes the ground as it moves and TIE fighter engines make an eerie wailing sound. Smaller Imperial vehicles are used for scouting and patrolling, while high-ranking officers travel in style aboard Star Destroyers and luxury Imperial Shuttles.

ALL TERRAIN ARMORED TRANSPORT (AT-AT)
- **SIZE** 22.5 m (73.8 ft) TALL
- **SPEED** 60 km/hr (37 mph)
- **CAPACITY** 3 CREW, 40 TROOPERS
- **WEAPONS** 2 HEAVY LASER CANNONS, 2 MEDIUM BLASTER CANNONS

ALL TERRAIN SCOUT TRANSPORT (AT-ST)
- **SIZE** 8.6 m (28.2 ft) TALL
- **SPEED** 90 km/hr (56 mph)
- **CAPACITY** 1 PILOT, 1 GUNNER
- **WEAPONS** 2 TWIN BLASTER CANNONS, 1 GRENADE LAUNCHER

COMMANDERS HAVE GOOD VIEW OF BATTLEFIELD

HEAVY ARMOR WITHSTANDS BLASTER FIRE

LEGS GIVE EXCELLENT MOVEMENT OVER UNEVEN SURFACES

HUGE FEET CRUSH ENEMIES

LAND

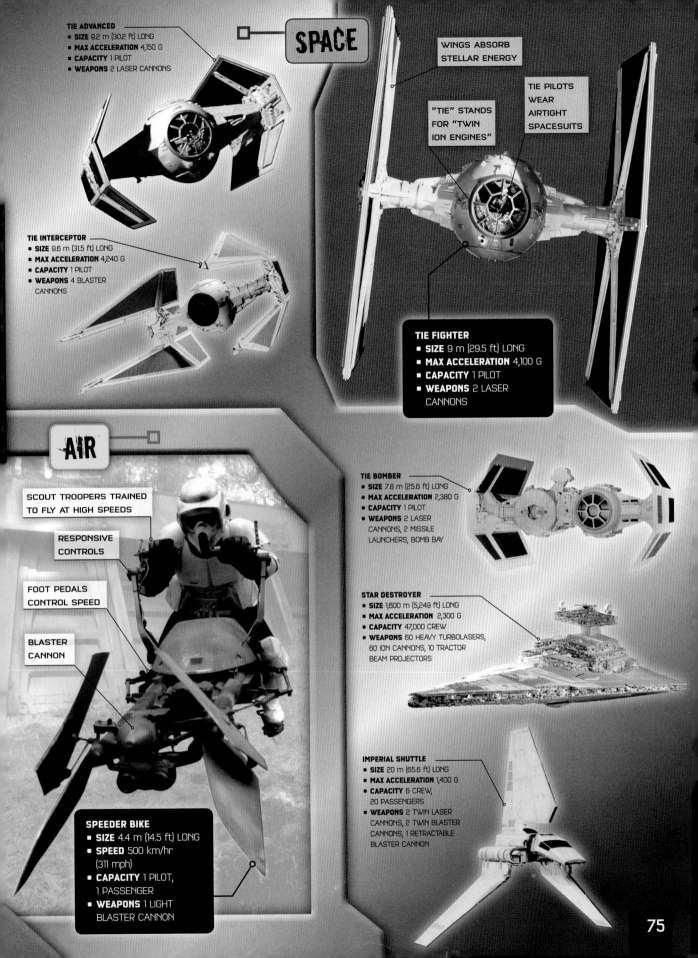

TIE ADVANCED
- **SIZE** 9.2 m (30.2 ft) LONG
- **MAX ACCELERATION** 4,150 G
- **CAPACITY** 1 PILOT
- **WEAPONS** 2 LASER CANNONS

SPACE

WINGS ABSORB STELLAR ENERGY

"TIE" STANDS FOR "TWIN ION ENGINES"

TIE PILOTS WEAR AIRTIGHT SPACESUITS

TIE INTERCEPTOR
- **SIZE** 9.6 m (31.5 ft) LONG
- **MAX ACCELERATION** 4,240 G
- **CAPACITY** 1 PILOT
- **WEAPONS** 4 BLASTER CANNONS

TIE FIGHTER
- **SIZE** 9 m (29.5 ft) LONG
- **MAX ACCELERATION** 4,100 G
- **CAPACITY** 1 PILOT
- **WEAPONS** 2 LASER CANNONS

AIR

SCOUT TROOPERS TRAINED TO FLY AT HIGH SPEEDS

RESPONSIVE CONTROLS

FOOT PEDALS CONTROL SPEED

BLASTER CANNON

TIE BOMBER
- **SIZE** 7.8 m (25.6 ft) LONG
- **MAX ACCELERATION** 2,380 G
- **CAPACITY** 1 PILOT
- **WEAPONS** 2 LASER CANNONS, 2 MISSILE LAUNCHERS, BOMB BAY

STAR DESTROYER
- **SIZE** 1,600 m (5,249 ft) LONG
- **MAX ACCELERATION** 2,300 G
- **CAPACITY** 47,000 CREW
- **WEAPONS** 60 HEAVY TURBOLASERS, 60 ION CANNONS, 10 TRACTOR BEAM PROJECTORS

IMPERIAL SHUTTLE
- **SIZE** 20 m (65.6 ft) LONG
- **MAX ACCELERATION** 1,400 G
- **CAPACITY** 6 CREW, 20 PASSENGERS
- **WEAPONS** 2 TWIN LASER CANNONS, 2 TWIN BLASTER CANNONS, 1 RETRACTABLE BLASTER CANNON

SPEEDER BIKE
- **SIZE** 4.4 m (14.5 ft) LONG
- **SPEED** 500 km/hr (311 mph)
- **CAPACITY** 1 PILOT, 1 PASSENGER
- **WEAPONS** 1 LIGHT BLASTER CANNON

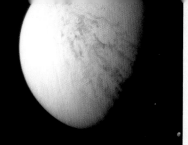

PLANET: Hoth

LOCATION: A remote sector of the Outer Rim Territories

TERRAIN: Glaciers, snow fields

INHABITANTS: Rebel Alliance soldiers, wampa ice monsters

ALLEGIANCE: Rebel Alliance

BATTLE ANALYSIS: HOTH

The Rebel Alliance has found a remote hideout for their new base. However, they know it's only a matter of time until the Empire tracks them down on the ice planet Hoth. The Rebels cannot win a battle against the better equipped Imperial troops, but they hope that they can hold off the Empire long enough to evacuate everyone on Echo Base to safety so they can live to fight another day.

"Imperial troops have entered the base!"

Rebel Trooper

1. PROBE DROID

OBJECTIVE:
Rebels to keep Echo Base hidden from the Empire.

OUTCOME:
Imperial probe droid spotted! Alarm is raised and evacuation begins. MISSION FAILED.

2. EVACUATION

OBJECTIVE:
All non-military personnel to escape Hoth.

OUTCOME:
Rebel transports jump into hyperspace. MISSION COMPLETE.

3. SNOW BATTLE

OBJECTIVE:
Rebel infantry and snowspeeders to delay the invading Imperial troops.

OUTCOME:
Rebels destroy some AT-ATs, but can't stop them all. MISSION INCOMPLETE.

4. SHIELD GENERATOR

OBJECTIVE:
Rebels to protect Echo Base's shield generator from Imperial attack.

OUTCOME:
An AT-AT blows up the generator, allowing more Imperial troops to land. MISSION FAILED.

5. ECHO BASE

OBJECTIVE:
Rebel troops to prevent Imperial snowtroopers from capturing the base.

OUTCOME:
Darth Vader and his troopers quickly take control. MISSION FAILED.

BATTLE STATS

EMPIRE:
- STAR DESTROYERS
- AT-ATS
- IMPERIAL OFFICERS AND SNOWTROOPERS
- WEAPONS: BLASTER RIFLES, AT-AT CHIN GUNS

REBEL ALLIANCE:
- DF.9 ANTI-INFANTRY BATTERIES
- P-TOWER LASER CANNONS
- T-47 AIRSPEEDERS
- REBEL GENERALS AND TROOPERS
- WEAPONS: BLASTER RIFLES

CONSEQUENCES

The Rebels escape after the Battle of Hoth, but they are badly hurt and weakened. Scattered and on the run from Imperial Star Destroyers, they regroup in deep space to plan their next move. The Empire looks stronger than ever, but the Rebels aren't discouraged. When the next battle comes, they will be ready!

6. ESCAPE

OBJECTIVE:
All remaining Rebels to abandon Echo Base and the Hoth system.

OUTCOME:
X-wings, transports, and the *Millennium Falcon* escape the battle. MISSION COMPLETE.

The snowspeeder's gunner fires a tow cable and the pilot loops his ship around the AT-AT's legs. Careful flying is needed or the snowspeeder might accidentally crash into the walking war machine!

HOW CAN YOU STOP AN AT-AT IN ITS TRACKS?

THE EMPIRE'S AT-AT WALKERS can destroy the Rebels with their blaster cannons and crush any survivors underneath their mechanical feet. The defending snowspeeders can't make a scratch in the walkers' heavy armor. It looks bad until Luke Skywalker comes up with a smart but risky idea—AT-ATs are giant-sized, but even the mightiest giant can topple and fall!

Its legs tangled, the AT-AT topples forward and crashes! A snowspeeder pilot takes aim at the damaged walker and hits a weak point in its neck. With a roar of fire the Imperial walker explodes, giving the Rebels more time to escape their base.

EXPLORING
REBEL BASES

The life of a Rebel soldier is an uncertain one. The Rebel Alliance can't match the Empire's firepower, so it needs to keep one step ahead of the enemy and be ready to escape at any time—day or night. The Alliance has already been forced to abandon its bases on Yavin 4 and Hoth, and now operates from the Mon Calamari Cruiser *Home One*—which uses hyperspace to stay on the move.

YAVIN 4
ABANDONED

Yavin 4 had many stone temples built by an ancient people called the Massassi. These pyramid-like structures were a good place to hide Rebel hangars and control rooms.

Technicians at the Yavin base constantly scanned the system for Imperial activity. They also worked hard to keep the X-wings and Y-wings in good condition in the jungle heat.

As a new Rebel recruit, it is crucial that you familiarize yourself with the layout of your base. You must learn every escape route—so you are prepared for an emergency evacuation.

ECHO BASE: NEW RECRUITS MAP

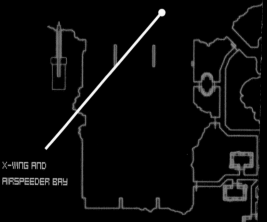

NORTH
ENTRANCE

X-WING AND
AIRSPEEDER BAY

WELCOME TO ECHO BASE. IMPORTANT LOCATIONS HAVE BEEN FLAGGED ON THE MAP. IF YOU HAVE ANY QUESTIONS I CAN BE FOUND IN THE CENTRAL COMMAND ROOM.
GOOD LUCK, SOLDIER

Major Kem Monnon

ECHO BASE

ABANDONED

The Echo Base hangar on Hoth was carved from solid ice. The Rebel speeders needed modification so they could operate in freezing temperatures.

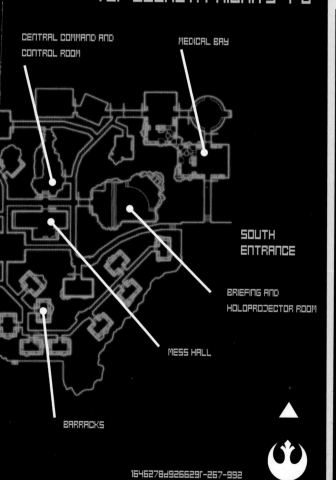

TOP SECRET: PRIORITY 4-B

CENTRAL COMMAND AND CONTROL ROOM

MEDICAL BAY

SOUTH ENTRANCE

BRIEFING AND HOLOPROJECTOR ROOM

MESS HALL

BARRACKS

1646278d926629r-267-992

Top Alliance officers are always scheduling meetings to plan military strategy. Rebel soldiers must never be captured, so you can never let your guard down.

Every Rebel base needs a medical center. Bacta tanks and surgical droids can heal most injuries and get Rebel soldiers back to the front lines.

HOME ONE

ACTIVE

Home One is the new mobile Rebel headquarters. It is protected by shields and turbolasers and it never stays in one place for long. In the briefing room, Imperial targets are displayed on holograms while soldiers and pilots receive their mission assignments.

CHAIN OF COMMAND

VILLAGE CHIEFTAIN
(CHIEF CHIRPA)

COUNCIL OF ELDERS

WAR CHIEFS

EWOK WARRIORS

UNLIKELY FRIENDS

Visitors to Endor's moon are rare, and Ewoks are suspicious of outsiders. At first they try to cook Han and Luke for dinner, but the Ewoks soon realize that the Rebels can help them keep their village safe from worse strangers.

In the dense forest of Endor, the Ewoks have a military advantage over the invading stormtroopers. They know every part of the terrain like the back of their paws, and they blend in with the forest colors.

Ewok WARRIORS

Ewoks may be small and furry, but watch out—these proud creatures can be fierce. The Ewoks don't know anything about the Galactic Civil War, but they do know that Imperial stormtroopers aren't welcome on their forest moon!

EWOK STATS

LEADER: CHIEF CHIRPA
ALLEGIANCE: REBEL ALLIANCE
HEADQUARTERS: BRIGHT TREE
VILLAGE, MOON OF ENDOR
WEAPONS: CATAPULTS, LOG TRAPS,
SNARES, ARROWS, SPEARS, BOLAS
VEHICLES: HANG GLIDERS,
WAR WAGONS
VALUES: TRIBAL LOYALTY,
PRESERVING NATURE

FIREPOWER
Ewok weapons and equipment made of wood, rope, and animal skins may look primitive, but with teamwork, the Ewoks are smart enough to defeat stormtroopers.

WISE LEADER
Chief Chirpa is the leader of the Ewoks who are drawn into war when their moon is chosen as the site for the Death Star's shield generator. Chirpa might not lead a trained army, but his tribe are brave, fierce, and determined to protect their home from the Empire.

HOODS ARE
A SIGN OF
ADULTHOOD

CHIEF CHIRPA

CHIRPA
BELIEVES THAT
HIS MEDALLION
HAS MYSTICAL
POWERS

CEREMONIAL
KNIFE IS A
SYMBOL OF
HIGH RANK

WICKET W. WARRICK

WICKET'S FAVORITE
WEAPONS ARE THE
SPEAR AND THE BOLA

INQUISITIVE SCOUT
Wicket is a scout who gets more than he expects when he finds Princess Leia in the forest. His curiosity is matched by his bravery in the Battle of Endor.

BATTLE ANALYSIS: ENDOR

MOON: Endor
LOCATION: A remote sector of the Outer Rim Territories
TERRAIN: Thick forests, treetop villages
INHABITANTS: Ewoks
ALLEGIANCE: None

After the Death Star is destroyed at the Battle of Yavin, the Empire builds a bigger, more powerful one! The Rebels plan to shut it down forever, but the battle station is protected by a shield, powered by a generator on the moon of Endor. A strike team lands on Endor to demolish the generator. Meanwhile, Lando Calrissian is standing by in the *Millennium Falcon*, waiting to attack the Death Star.

1. CAPTURED

OBJECTIVE:
Han Solo, Princess Leia, and Chewbacca to destroy the shield generator.

OUTCOME:
The trio realize they have walked into a trap and are captured. MISSION FAILED.

2. SPACE BATTLE

OBJECTIVE:
Rebels to defeat Imperial warships near the Death Star.

OUTCOME:
Rebels destroy Imperial ships but take heavy losses too. MISSION INCOMPLETE.

BATTLE STATS

EMPIRE:
- SITH
- IMPERIAL OFFICERS AND STORMTROOPERS
- DEATH STAR
- STAR DESTROYERS
- AT-STS

REBEL ALLIANCE:
- JEDI
- EWOK WARRIORS
- REBEL TROOPS
- MON CALAMARI CRUISERS
  - BTL Y-WINGS
  - T-65 X-WINGS
  - A-WINGS
  - B-WINGS
  - *MILLENNIUM FALCON*

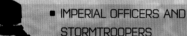

3. LAND BATTLE

OBJECTIVE:
Rebels to fight their way out of the Imperial trap.

OUTCOME:
Ewoks join the fight and beat the soldiers with spears and rocks. MISSION COMPLETE.

4. DEATH STAR DUEL

OBJECTIVE:
Luke Skywalker to defeat Darth Vader and the Emperor.

OUTCOME:
Darth Vader throws the Emperor into a shaft to save Luke. MISSION COMPLETE.

> "The shield is down! Commence attack on the Death Star's **MAIN REACTOR.**"
>
> Admiral Ackbar

5. SHIELD GENERATOR

OBJECTIVE:
Strike team to destroy the shield protecting the Death Star.

OUTCOME:
This time, the generator explodes. MISSION COMPLETE.

6. DESTROY DEATH STAR

OBJECTIVE:
Lando to trigger an explosion in the Death Star's main reactor.

OUTCOME:
With the shield down, Lando blasts the core. MISSION COMPLETE.

CONSEQUENCES

The Battle of Endor is a great victory for the Rebel Alliance and the people of the galaxy. Celebrations are held from Coruscant to Tatooine to cheer the end of the Empire and the start of a new era of peace. Luke Skywalker is the last of the Jedi, but he can now re-establish the Jedi Order.

HOW CAN A SMALL ARMY TAKE ON THE EMPIRE?

ARMED ONLY WITH logs and rope, the Ewoks are up against the strongest army in the galaxy! But the Imperial Army is on unfamiliar ground, so when C-3PO leads them into an ambush, the clever little Ewoks show why they should never be underestimated!

A distracted enemy is a weakened enemy! A sneaky Ewok warrior steals a speeder bike and leads Imperial scout troopers on a wild chase. Now there are fewer guards at the Rebels' real target—the shield generator bunker.

The Ewoks might not have sophisticated weapons, but they know how to fight in a forest. Their catapults can dent AT-ST armor, and rolling logs can make the walkers slip and fall. And two tree trunks, released at just the right moment, can crush an AT-ST like an egg!

MISSION DATA

■ The Empire knew about the Ewoks when it chose Endor as the location of the new Death Star project, but it believed Ewoks were too small and simple to be a threat.

A lifelong gambler, Lando knows when to stand and when to walk away. Admiral Ackbar wants to retreat, but Lando suggests fighting the Star Destroyers to buy more time.

HOW DO YOU TURN AROUND A
LOSING BATTLE?

IT'S A TRAP! The Rebel Alliance's sneak attack has failed and Imperial forces are now battle ready. The Rebels are vastly outnumbered both in space and on the moon of Endor. It looks hopeless. But Lando Calrissian has faith in his friends; working together, the Rebels still have a chance to bring down the Empire.

Lando never doubts that Han Solo and his team will destroy the Death Star's shield generator. When news of their success on Endor's moon comes through, Lando's delaying strategy pays off and the real attack on the now vulnerable Death Star begins!

SMALL BATTLES
CAN MAKE A BIG DIFFERENCE

What causes the Empire's defeat? In the end, it is a son's love for his father. Luke Skywalker never gives up hope, and he convinces Darth Vader to turn back to the light side of the Force. Like a row of falling dominoes, this compassionate act leads to the defeat of the Emperor and freedom for the entire galaxy.

LUKE SKYWALKER ESCAPES
Luke defeats Vader in a lightsaber duel, but the battle isn't over! The Emperor tries to turn Luke to the dark side, but Luke's willpower is strong and he resists.

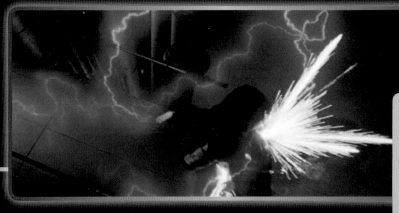

DEATH OF AN EMPEROR
Furious, the Emperor fires Force lightning at Luke. Vader sees his son in pain and comes to his rescue. With his last bit of strength, Vader throws his Master into a deep pit.

THE EMPIRE'S COLLAPSE
Without their leader, everything goes wrong for the Imperial forces. Rebel starfighters take down the Empire's Super Star Destroyer and a ground team on Endor blows up the shield generator. Soon, the mighty Death Star suffers a critical hit to its main reactor and explodes.

THE SITH ARE DESTROYED
Now that the Emperor is dead and Darth Vader has turned away from the dark side of the Force, the Sith no longer rule the galaxy. Luke Skywalker can now turn the Jedi Order into the guardians of peace and justice once more.

THE RETURN OF ANAKIN SKYWALKER
Luke always believed that deep down, Darth Vader still had the good spirit of Anakin Skywalker. Vader is dying from his injuries but he is at peace. He tells Luke, "You were right about me."

REBEL ALLIANCE VICTORY
Across the galaxy, planets celebrate the Empire's downfall. For the Rebels it has been a long, hard fight, but by working together they have triumphed!

...THE JEDI ORDER LIVES ON...

91

GLOSSARY

ASTROMECH DROID
- A utility robot that repairs and helps navigate starships.

BATTLE DROID
- A Separatist robot designed for combat.

BATTLE OF CORUSCANT
- Clone Wars conflict in 19 BBY where the Separatist army attacks the planet Coruscant, kidnapping Supreme Chancellor Palpatine.

BATTLE OF ENDOR
- Conflict in 4 ABY where the Rebel Alliance attacks Imperial forces on the moon of Endor, resulting in the destruction of the second Death Star and marking the decline of the Empire.

BATTLE OF GEONOSIS
- Conflict in 22 BBY where the Republic's clone army attacks the Separatists' battle droid army on the planet Geonosis, marking the start of the Clone Wars.

BATTLE OF HOTH
- Conflict in 3 ABY where Imperial forces attack Rebel headquarters Echo Base on the planet Hoth.

BATTLE OF KASHYYYK
- Conflict in 19 BBY where the Separatists' droid army fights against the Wookiees and Jedi on the planet Kashyyyk.

BATTLE OF NABOO
- Conflict in 32 BBY where the Trade Federation invades the planet Naboo with their battle droid army.

BATTLE OF YAVIN
- Conflict in Year 0 where Rebel forces, based on the moon Yavin 4, attack and destroy the first Imperial Death Star.

BLOCKADE
- A political strategy that prevents food and resources from reaching a specific destination.

BOLA
- A throwing weapon made up of a rope with stones at each end.

BOUNTY HUNTER
- Someone who tracks down, captures, or kills wanted people in exchange for money.

BUZZ DROIDS
- Small droids that latch onto and sabotage enemy spacecraft; often used by Separatist forces in space battles.

CHANCELLOR
- The title given to the head of the Galactic Senate and Republic.

CLONE ARMY
- An army of genetically identical soldiers, all trained to be perfect warriors. They fight for the Republic.

CLONE WARS
- A series of galaxy-wide battles fought between the Republic's clone army and the droid army of the Confederacy of Independent Systems, which took place between 22 and 19 BBY.

CYBORG
- A being that is partly a living organism and partly a robot.

DARK SIDE
- The evil side of the Force that feeds off negative emotions and offers raw power to those who study it.

DEATH STAR
- A planet-sized battle station built by the Empire which has enough firepower to destroy an entire planet.

DEMOCRACY
- A system of government where all senior politicians are elected by the population.

DROIDEKA
- A destroyer droid used in battle by the Separatists.

ELECTROSTAFF
- Weapon favored by General Grievous and his MagnaGuard bodyguards.

EMPEROR

■ Ruler of the Empire.

EMPIRE

■ A tyrannical power that rules the galaxy from 19 BBY to 4 ABY under the leadership of the Emperor, who is a Sith Lord.

FAMBAA

■ Four-legged creature used by the Gungan Army to support their shield generators.

FORCE

■ The energy that flows through all living things, which can used for either good or evil.

FORCE LIGHTNING

■ Deadly rays of blue energy that can be used as a weapon by someone who has embraced the dark side of the Force.

GALACTIC CIVIL WAR

■ Conflict between 2 BBY and 4 ABY in which the Rebel Alliance opposes and fights against the Galactic Empire.

GRAND MASTER

■ The leader of the Jedi Council.

GUNGANS

■ An amphibious species from the planet Naboo.

JEDI

■ An ancient sect of Force-sensitives who study the light side and use their powers for the good of the galaxy.

JEDI COUNCIL

■ The 12 senior, respected members of the Jedi Order who meet to make important decisions and give advice.

JEDI KNIGHT

■ A member of the Jedi Order who has studied as a Padawan under a Jedi Master and has passed the Jedi Trials.

JEDI MASTER

■ A rank for Jedi Knights who have performed an exceptional deed or have trained a Jedi Knight.

JEDI ORDER

■ An ancient organization that promotes peace and justice throughout the galaxy.

JEDI PURGE

■ The attempt by Chancellor Palpatine in 19 BBY to annihilate the entire Jedi Order.

JEDI TEMPLE

■ The headquarters of the Jedi Order, located on the planet Coruscant.

KAADU

■ Loyal, gentle creatures native to Naboo. Gungan soldiers use them as mounts in battle.

KAMA

■ A protective addition to clone trooper armor, worn around the waist.

KAMINO

■ A stormy, ocean planet on which the clone army was built, located beyond the Outer Rim.

KASHYYYK

■ A jungle planet where the Wookiees live, located in the Mid Rim.

LIGHTSABER

■ A weapon with a blade of pure energy that is used by Jedi and Sith warriors.

ORDER 66

■ An order given by Chancellor Palpatine that begins the Jedi Purge. Every trooper in the clone army is ordered to kill all the Jedi.

PADAWAN

■ A Youngling who is chosen to serve an apprenticeship with a Jedi Master.

PODRACING

■ A popular sport in which competitors race against each other in high-powered vehicles.

PROBE DROID

■ Imperial robot that gathers and transmits data.

REBEL ALLIANCE

■ The organization that resists and fights against the Empire.

REPUBLIC

■ The long-standing government of the galaxy, under leadership of an elected Chancellor.

SENATE

■ Government of the Republic, with representatives from all parts of the galaxy.

SENATOR

■ A person who represents their planet, sector, or system in the Senate.

SEPARATISTS

■ An alliance against the Republic. Also known as the Confederacy of Independent Systems.

SITH

■ An ancient sect of Force-sensitives who study the dark side to gain control and succeed in their greedy plans.

TRADE FEDERATION

■ A bureaucratic organization that controls much of the trade and commerce in the galaxy.

YOUNGLING

■ A Force-sensitive child who joins the Jedi Order to be trained in the Jedi arts.

INDEX

Characters are listed under their most frequently used common name, for example Luke Skywalker is found under "L" and "Count Dooku" is under "C."

Main entries are in bold.

LONDON, NEW YORK, MELBOURNE,
MUNICH, AND DELHI

For Dorling Kindersley

EDITOR Shari Last
SENIOR EDITOR Elizabeth Dowsett
DESIGNER Toby Truphet
ADDITIONAL DESIGN BY Rob Perry,
Mark Richards, Rhys Thomas
MANAGING ART EDITOR Ron Stobbart
PUBLISHING MANAGER Catherine Saunders
ART DIRECTOR Lisa Lanzarini
ASSOCIATE PUBLISHER Simon Beecroft
CATEGORY PUBLISHER Alex Allan
PRODUCTION EDITOR Sean Daly
PRODUCTION CONTROLLER Nick Seston

JACKET DESIGN BY Lynne Moulding

For Lucasfilm

EXECUTIVE EDITOR J. W. Rinzler
ART DIRECTOR Troy Alders
KEEPER OF THE HOLOCRON Leland Chee
DIRECTOR OF PUBLISHING Carol Roeder

First published in the United States in 2011
by DK Publishing
375 Hudson Street, New York, New York 10014

11 12 13 14 15   10 9 8 7 6 5 4 3 2 1
178199—01/11

DK books are available at special discounts when purchased in
bulk for sales promotions, premiums, fund-raising, or educational use.
For details, contact: DK Publishing Special Markets,
375 Hudson Street, New York, New York 10014. SpecialSales@dk.com

A catalog record for this book is
available from the Library of Congress.

ISBN: 978-0-7566-7315-4

Color reproduction by Media Development Printing Ltd.
Printed and bound in Singapore by Star Standard.

The publisher would like to thank Julia March for
her editorial assistance and Alastair Dougall for the index.

Discover more at
www.dk.com
www.starwars.com